A DICTI CONTEMPORARY CHRISTIAN WORDS AND CONCEPTS

Michael Pitts

insight *i* publishing group

A Dictionary of Contemporary Christian Words and Concepts by Michael Pitts

Published by Insight Publishing Group
8801 S. Yale, Suite 410
Tulsa, OK 74137
918-493-1718

Unless otherwise noted, all Scripture quotations are from the King James Version of the Bible or the New King James Version of the Bible. Copyright © 1979, 1980, 1982 by Thomas Nelson Inc., publishers. Used by permission.

Cover design by Jeffrey Mobley

For more information and other product materials contact
Cornerstone Church
PO Box 351690
Toledo, OH 43635
(419) 725-5000
www.cornerstonetoledo.com

ISBN 1-930027-20-6
Library of Congress catalog card number: 2001086732

Printed in the United States of America

Abase. The relegating of a person or thing to a lower level than is truly occupied. When applied to a person, it especially involves purposeful or ignorant words and actions to put another down. On many occasions, especially when purposeful, actions may seek to provoke in people insecurity and feelings of self-doubt, making people feel lowered.

Abba. A term of endearment for God the Father.

Abide. The act of continual dwelling.

Abomination. Speaks of something that is openly scandalous or offensive to God.

Abundance. More than enough.

Acceptable. Something that is proper. Something that is offered becomes acceptable when one of greater authority says that it is proper. For example, Romans 12 says, "I beseech you therefore brethren by the mercies of God that you present your bodies as a living sacrifice, holy and *acceptable* unto God which is your reasonable service" (emphasis added). For something to be acceptable, it has to first be presented, and then the recipient must accept it as proper. Every offering is not necessarily acceptable. Every song that is sung is not necessarily acceptable. This carries with it the concept that a Christian must live his or her life in a way that is acceptable to God.

A

Accord. Agreement. To be of the same mind. The concurring of opinion and will. To be in the same flow, direction, mindset, and disposition as another.

Accountable. Being in the position of giving account to another. The posture of being subject to answer to higher authority. To report to another on a given task.

Accuser of brethren. Accuser comes from *a cursor.* It is another name that is given to Satan. It is his position, where he stands before God day and night accusing the brethren. Accusing, *a cursing,* means to stand in the face of God and to actually accuse, to say, "Look, this is what they did; this is what they have done."

Activate. To bring to life and to set in motion something in someone else.

Activation. The process, given set of circumstances, or method employed to activate another. It may include but is not limited to the laying on of hands, association over time, the receiving of a divine truth through preaching and teaching, prophetic utterance, or being in an atmosphere of faith.

Adam. There is a first Adam and a last Adam. The first Adam is the man named Adam, who was created in Genesis. He is the fountainhead of the human race, the natural man. The last Adam is a term used in reference to Christ. The Bible discusses how man, as the first Adam, died and how Christ, as the last Adam, was made alive. What Adam lost, Christ regained.

A

Adultery. A sexual relationship with a married person outside the covenant of marriage. It is different from fornication in that fornication involves single people having a sexual relationship. Adultery means that one or both of the people are married to someone else.

Adversary. One who is set in opposition against.

Affirmation. The positive building up of one who is doing right by recognizing it and validating it.

Agape. One of the distinctions of the word *love.* Agape refers to the God kind of love. It is used to describe the kind of love that God has toward you. Unconditional and spiritual, agape love is showing to another person the same kind of love that God has shown to you. (For *phileo* and *eros*, see Love.)

Age. The length of time in which something has its greatest import and impact (Church Age, Apostolic Age, etc.). It is noted by fulfillment and fruition of divine purpose.

Agreement. Coming into line with another by being, thinking, feeling, or positioning the same way on a particular matter.

Ahab Spirit. From the Bible story of Ahab and Jezebel, the Ahab Spirit may be defined as the abandonment of responsibility by allowing someone of lesser authority to take over areas of responsibility for which they are not suited. This usually occurs as a result of weakness and inability to maintain responsibility for one's self in the face of the lesser authority's demands for power and control. The Ahab Spirit frequently functions in male/female

A

relationships, and there may be seduction and the filling of perceived needs involved. The Ahab Spirit should *not* be confused with delegation of authority, for it is truly the abdicating of authority.

Alienation. The feeling of not belonging and of being isolated and alone.

Alignment. Refers to positioning one's self in agreement with another or others. It is the position of being in agreement with other people—those with whom you are aligned. It also is a term used for the corrective application of the Word or for someone's speaking to you and causing things in your life to come into proper order. That may mean you have pieces that are there, but you are just a little askew in thinking, feeling, or attitude and need to be brought into proper alignment.

Alleluia. Alleluia means to hallow the name of God, and it can be spelled either *alleluia* or *hallelujah*. Interestingly, it is one of the only words that are pronounced the same in every language of the world. Hallelujah begins with hal-le-lu and ends with j-h-a, which is *ya,* as in Yahweh and Jehovah.

Alliance. To make an alliance is to make an agreement with or to come into agreement. It is stronger than just agreeing because you can agree with someone you are not aligned with. An alliance involves the intentional joining of forces to accomplish something. It is to align and to join forces with a particular person, ideology, or movement.

Almighty. A name that people use to refer to God and His omnipotence.

Altar. A place of sacrifice and a place of exchange. Sacrifices are put on the altar, so the altar, therefore, is a place of exchange. It is also the term used in many churches for the designated area at the front of the sanctuary where people come to pray. It implies coming to pray with the mentality that you are laying something down, that you are coming for exchange between God and yourself, and that you are coming to sacrifice and to worship. The altar is the place that is commonly used for people to come and to pray to receive Christ.

Altar call. An altar call is the giving of an invitation and the subsequent response by people as they physically and publicly respond in prayer and in person to the message that they have heard. It is most generally referred to as becoming born again, but it may also include prayer for healing, deliverance, the receiving of the Holy Spirit, or special blessings.

Altar worker. Altar workers are individuals who have been assigned to help those coming with various needs for prayer at the altar. (See Ministry of helps.)

Amen. Means "so be it." It is a verbal response signifying agreement with what has been spoken.

Angels. Created spirit beings. They are the messengers of God. They operate at God's command and do not have their own agendas. The Bible says that they are ministers to the heirs of salvation. They work on behalf of the prayers of Christians. All angels are positive. Their

A

counterparts are demons, which are fallen angels. The Bible says that angels are innumerable.

Anointing. Anointing is the divine empowerment to do. Anointing in a certain context can be defined as discerning the presence of God. It is not so much a feeling as it is discernment. It is given by the Holy Spirit. For a person to walk in an anointing, there needs to be a yieldedness on the inside of them. They begin to work purposely with God's impetus in their lives. They are, therefore, able to accomplish things with greater ease than they could have on their own.

Anointing, law of. When a person functions under the anointing, burdens are lifted and yokes are destroyed. For example, one person can be a technically proficient and wonderful singer. When this person gets up, he or she sings on pitch and on cue, and it is beautiful and people enjoy it. Another person gets up and may not sing as well, but as he or she sings burdens are lifted and yokes are destroyed. That person is anointed. (See Anointing.)

Answer. An answer implies that there was an internal question or questioning—especially within a person who at some moment comes to realize or to understand the meaning of something or what should be done about something. It is cognitive, not just handed to people, when they realize that they have gotten their answer. A person can answer an altar call, as in the following: We want you to respond to this call. In that respect, answer means to acknowledge by action.

Apostate. Forsaking truth and living in and promoting false doctrine.

Apostle. Comes from the word *sent*. *Apostolos* is the actual Greek. Being an apostle is one of the five-fold ministry gifts. It is a governing gift in the body of Christ. In I Corinthians 12:28, it is listed as the first among the offices that are set in the church. It is the first in order, rank, and importance. It carries with it a revelatory grace. It is a governing gift in the body, helping to direct the other ministry gifts. It is a doctrinal gift. It is a foundational gift. Apostles are overseers. There are world apostles and regional apostles. Apostles are people who have authority and grace given to them by God in a particular region. There are also local apostles. They are groundbreakers. They are pioneers. Apostles don't require someone else's foundation to build upon. They can go into a hostile climate and begin to break open entire areas, bring new understanding, release new spiritual truths, gather people, and build them up. Apostles establish them; it is an establishing gift. They bring people into establishment and authority. Apostles are builders; they build people. They take a group of people and make them into a church.

Apostles of the Lamb. The distinction given to the twelve disciples who became apostles and walked with Jesus while He was alive in His earthly ministry.

Appropriate. To appropriate means to take, apply, and move something into your own account. For example, every work of grace has to be appropriated. God has given salvation; it is yours to receive. You have to appropriate salvation by faith. You have to receive it into your

A

account through faith. God's desire is for everyone to be blessed. You appropriate blessing by tithing. That appropriates blessing into your account. Your appropriations are what your believing and your corresponding action make yours—not in a technical sense but experientially.

Archangels. The highest-ranking classification of angels. Three archangels were mentioned in the Bible: Michael, Gabriel, and Lucifer. Lucifer, who at his fall became Satan, left Michael and Gabriel. The number of archangels is fixed at three. There is a concept that there are three archangels because each one of them is directly associated with, and has been delegated authority under, a particular person of the Godhead. Their names give bearing to that. Michael means *who is like God.* Generally, Michael is sent from God the Father. Gabriel is the one with the message. He always has the trumpet, which is symbolic of a message, and he usually comes to bring a message of the Holy Spirit because the Holy Spirit is the messenger. Lucifer means *son of the morning.* Jesus is the morning star. There is a concept that this is why the Word of God, Jesus, came to redeem man: Jesus may have come because Lucifer, while under Jesus' authority, was the archangel that fell and took a third of the angels.

Ark of the Covenant. The Ark of the Covenant was the ark, a wooden box overlaid and inlaid with gold, that the priests of the children of Israel carried with them on their shoulders as a reminder of their covenant, and in which the presence of God dwelled. It contained Aaron's rod that budded, the unbroken tablets of stone on which the Ten Commandments were written, and a golden pot of manna.

Armor. Putting on armor means to fortify yourself or to spiritually equip yourself for a particular battle. There is a reference in Ephesians 6 having to do with putting on the whole armor of God.

Armorbearer. In ancient days when people would go off to battle, warriors had people who traveled with them to carry their armor so that their strength was not used up in carrying it themselves. This way they would be more effective when the battle came. The word *armorbearer* has to do with people who are assigned to and make themselves available to those of greater authority. They do whatever natural thing they can in order to lift the load of someone in authority so that the person in authority can be more effective in the spiritual dimension. (See Forward untangling.)

Asceticism. The denial of natural or physical desires and pleasures in the hopes of obtaining spiritual enlightenment or betterment.

Assembly. A particular group of people that has come together in some form or fashion; believers.

Assigned spirits and spiritual assassins. This is the concept that individuals, families, churches, groups of people, races, or even whole nations have particular spirits that are assigned to them. These spirits generally remain undetected throughout life and sabotage success at moments of promotion. The terms *assignment* and *assassination* are used because there is a correlation to the way that these spirits operate. You are seldom assassinated until you are in a high-ranking office. If assassins are going to wait to take someone out, they must

A

remain undetected. These spirits will remain undetected while working in a person. They will push a person to the brink of destruction and then release the pressure so that the person does not delve any further to find out what the root problem is. You will see cyclical patterns of failure in a person's life. You may see that every time things are about to go well in some people's lives, the same problems come back again. This is the indication that there are assigned spirits at work. These spirits are there to assassinate the person's potential and opportunity. They are assigned to people by the devil. Their assignment, their function in life, is to be with a person and to work on him or her. Sometimes they begin early in childhood and stay with people all through life until the assignment is done. The assignment is their purpose, and their purpose is to assassinate; therefore, *assassin* is the term given to the spirit itself.

Atonement. Atonement is doing something to correct a previous wrong so as to bring *at-one-ment;* to bring together two things that were divided.

Authority. Authority and power go together due to the words from which they come: *exousia,* which means *authority*, and *dunamis*, which means *power. Dunamis* is where the word dynamite originates. *Dunamis* is ability, and it can be divine or natural. You can say that you have the *power* to move something. It is the ability to do. *Exousia* then is the authority to exercise that power. Conversely, *dunamis* is the power that backs up the authority. There is authority that backs up power, and there is power that backs up authority. For example, a police officer who witnesses a crime holds up his *exousia*, his badge. He says, "Stop in the name of the law." If you don't stop, he pulls his *dunamis* from the holster. One is the authority, and the other one is the power. They work interchangeably because sometimes a police officer can stand in the middle of the street and can hold his hand up to stop an eighteen-wheeler—not by power but by authority. So one is the ability to do something, and the other is the authority to do it. *Authority* is also a generic term used to describe all those who are in charge of something. You may say to someone, "Before you do that, check with authority." (See Bind, Headship, and Measure of authority.)

Awe. In the Christian reference, awe is wonder.

Azusa. Azusa is the name of the street in Southern California where an outpouring of the Holy Spirit came at the onset of the twentieth century. Most spirit-filled denominations came from that experience. The actual address is 312 Azusa Street, Los Angeles, California.

.

Baby dedication. Commonly practiced in Protestant churches as distinct from infant baptism. In most Protestant churches, infants are not baptized, but they are dedicated. It is any form of various ceremonies involving the acknowledgment that the child has come as a gift from God. It includes the promissory position of those present to do their best to raise that child in the ways of God.

Babylon. There is the physical place, but Babylon is also used as a reference to something that is evil. It has a negative connotation of something that is antichrist and worldly.

Backslide. To purposely return to a former lifestyle. To backslide, you have to come to a particular point of understanding in your life, turn your back on it, and walk away from the truth that you received and to which you subscribed.

Baptism into Christ. Baptism means immersion. It comes from the word *baptismo,* which means *to immerse.* This is an important distinction because what many churches refer to as a baptism is not a baptism by definition. If you have water poured on your head, you have not been baptized; you have merely had water poured on your head. By definition, the word *baptism* means *to be immersed into something.* That is an important distinction historically and theologically for particular reasons. Baptism into Christ means to be immersed into Christ.

B

Baptism is done in the name of Jesus. It actually means *into*. You are being baptized into the name of Jesus, which means that you are being baptized into what that name represents. You are being baptized into the body of Christ. It is symbolic of being buried with Christ and then being raised up in the newness of life.

Baptism of the Holy Spirit. The baptism of the Holy Spirit is being immersed into the Holy Spirit. The baptism of the Holy Spirit is a definite work of grace subsequent to salvation. When you are born again, you have the indwelling of the Spirit, which takes place when God sends His Spirit into your heart to testify that you are a child of God. But after that, the baptism of the Holy Spirit comes, which is the *infilling* of the Spirit rather than the *indwelling* of the Spirit. What is the difference? It is the difference between a well and a river. The *indwelling* of the Spirit is for you; it is like a well, which provides water in one location only. The *infilling* of the Spirit empowers you to do something for someone else; it is like a river, which flows between many points.

Baptism of water. To the born-again Christian, baptism is an outward sign of an inward work. It says, "I now want to be identified with the body of Christ." It is symbolic of the newness of life. Water is symbolic of the water's breaking during a birth. You come out into newness of life. Baptism is a conscious decision.

Barren. Lack of production and lack of reproduction. In the spiritual sense, it implies a spirit, a geographical region, or a particular people who, after having the seed of the Word of God and the impartation of ministry given to them, still do not reproduce what they have heard.

They don't come to an understanding of God, or they don't turn around and spread the Word of God. The Word just doesn't do anything for them. They are barren. They have heard it repeatedly, but there is no evidence of that in their lives.

Battle. A battle is a conflict. A battle takes place when two forces have defined lines and are engaged. It is the engagement of opposing forces and positions. Your ideas and fellow employee's ideas can be in conflict, but there is a difference between that and a battle. A battle refers to those things coming into proximity and actually engaging in warfare.

Belief. Something that someone adheres to. Adhering to a belief does not necessarily make it right or wrong. It is not a conclusion. Belief is a level of certainty that does not rise to the level of knowledge. It is something of which you feel certain, no matter whether it is right or wrong, with or without substantiating facts, but you may not have necessarily come to the point of proving it. You may not be able to objectively support your belief when explaining it to someone else. Belief is something that one accepts as being true.

Bewitched. To have someone else's actions or thoughts ensnare you. It is akin to a soul tie, but a soul tie has a lot to do with relationship. Bewitching can happen more casually. (See Soul tie.)

Bind. Bind and loose are usually linked together in the Bible. Whatsoever you bind on earth is bound in heaven, and whatsoever you loose on earth is loosed in heaven. The measurability of your authority is based on the speed and the scope at which you can initiate and prohibit; it is based on what you can start into motion and what you can stop from being in motion. To loose is to initiate and start. To bind is to prohibit and stop. (See Authority.)

Birth or birthing. This is the counterpart to barren. It is bringing out of your spirit something that will manifest itself in the natural realm.

Birthright. Generally applied to the first-born. The first-born has the birthright blessing, the inheritance so to speak. The birthright blessing is sometimes referred to as the double portion. In the Old Testament, the first-born legally received the double portion. The first-born received all of the immovable property and anything under the father's authority at the time of his passing. The other children could pull the wagons off the land and take the cattle, but the first-born inherited all of the ground, the real estate under the father's possession. In addition, the first-born received a double portion of all the other birthrights, not just real estate.

The spiritual birthright is exemplified by Elijah and Elisha, who were not connected by genealogy. However, Elisha did refer to Elijah as his spiritual father. Before Elijah was taken from earth, he asked Elisha, "What do you want?"

Elisha said, "I want a double portion of your spirit." The spiritual birthright refers to transference of spirit, transference of anointing; the double portion anointing was given to Elisha. Everything that Elijah had conquered, all of the ground and space that he had moved into in his life, went to the person who had followed him, Elisha. The last miracle of Elijah was the first miracle of Elisha. The principle of the double portion refers to your starting where somebody else left off. A father gives the birthright to his first-born to start where the father finished. The heir has two portions: the one received from the father and the one made on his own.

Bishop. Originates from the word *epi* and the word *scopes*. *Scopes* refers to the word *scope*, to see. *Epi* means over, or oversight. Bishop, therefore, means to see over; a bishop is an overseer. It is essentially a ranking in a hierarchy.

Bitterness. A state of being when perceived wrongs and distraught feelings have taken root in a person, have become hardened, and have kept that person from experiencing joy, peace, and blessing. (See Spirit of offense.)

Blasting. A term used to describe confrontational preaching that is used for a spiritual effect. It is metaphoric and refers to opening up an area. For example, before a house can be built, trees may have to be blasted out, cleared, or cut down. It is clearing a space by strong preaching.

Blessing. This word has three aspects. Blessed means to speak well of. You can bless someone by speaking well of him or her. You can say, "God bless you." Blessed also means to set apart for a specific purpose or to sanctify. A church is a blessed place, not because the brick or the carpet is any different but because it is set apart for a specific godly purpose. The third definition is to prosper someone or to help someone in his or her journey. When

B

God said to Abraham, "I will bless you," He was saying, "I will help you in your journey." There is a difference between *the* blessing and *a* blessing. Someone could give you a tie, and you would refer to that as a nice blessing; however, *the* blessing is the favor of God.

Blindness. The inability to see. Metaphorically, blindness is a term that is attached to those who have no spiritual perception.

Blood of Jesus. There was, of course, the actual, physical blood of Jesus. The blood of Jesus is distinct due to an understanding that goes back to the book of Leviticus, which says that the life of the flesh is in the blood. Blood is more than just biological functioning. There is something of the person, which is carried through the blood. Sometimes characteristics beyond the physical and biological are passed through the bloodline. But Jesus came born of a woman and conceived by the Holy Spirit. Therefore, His blood is without the taint or stain of original sin. This is a construction that goes all the way back to the children of Israel who came out of Egypt at the Passover. The last plague poured out upon Egypt was the death of the first-born. The children of Israel were instructed to find a lamb without spot or blemish, to shed the blood of that lamb, and to put it over the doorpost of their house. When the destroyer came by, God said, "I will pass over the door of your house, and I will not allow the destroyer into your house." The Biblical concept referred to here is a type and a shadow, which means that something is not the substance itself but a type that foreshadows something to come later. When Jesus came, John said, "Behold the Lamb of God who takes away the sins of the world." So

Jesus was foreshadowed by the lamb whose blood was shed at Passover, and He is metaphorically applied to the doorpost of our house so that the destroyer cannot enter. When people say, "I plead the blood of Jesus," they are saying, "I want what His blood purchased for me to happen on my behalf."

Bloodline. Has to do with lineage. It refers to whom you are related through blood.

Board. A group of people much like a committee. This group of people is used in some church structures as a ruling and governing power, generally over practical matters.

Body. The body is the corporal, material, temporary vessel that houses the spirit and soul.

Body ministry. This is the concept that every person in the church has a place. The body ministry more specifically is the body of the church ministering to itself in different forms and fashions, especially in relation to headship ministries. This means that the pastors or the five-fold ministry is not doing it. A body ministry, for example, includes altar workers praying for people, children's teachers teaching the children, and members praying one for another. Intercession is a part of the body ministry. Body ministry is not done by those in headship. (See Ministry of helps.)

Bold in the Lord. This term means to be confident, unashamed, and forward, but not offensive or obtrusive in your convictions.

B

Boldness. It does not mean crass or rude. And it doesn't imply that you need to be disrespectful. It is the position of being confident and assured to do what you believe, and it means to do and say what is in your heart.

Bondage. A life of sin or the confining residue left from sin that restricts freedom.

Bondwoman. One who became married out of law, rather than out of love. It is the word picture or understanding of a relationship that comes not from love or covenant but rather from legalism. It comes from the Old Testament, in which it referred to a man with two wives; one was a bondwoman, who was legally his, and the other was the wife, which he loved. It becomes a word picture of the Old Covenant church and the New Covenant church. The Old Covenant church was the bondwoman because it was a relationship totally outlined by legalistic principles. And figuratively, the wife of love is the New Covenant church.

Born again. Used to define conversion or repentance. It is also being born from above. It is the state of the spirit being recreated.

Born of above. Means of above, of the higher nature. It is being born of the Spirit. It is being born from the higher nature, being born again.

Bound. Refers to someone who is not free. That someone has a strong hindrance in a particular area, a lack of freedom.

Bread. There is the natural definition, which is something made from flour. It is also a word picture of something that is a staple, something that you need in order to have nourishment and to survive. Jesus said, "I am the Bread of Life. If any man is hungry let him eat of me." Bread in the natural sense is physical sustenance, and bread in the spiritual sense speaks of sustenance at the spiritual level. Bread does not just mean bread. It does not mean just the wheat product. It means the whole sustenance of life, the things we need naturally to live, and the spiritual things we need.

Breakthrough. Occurs at the point of the greatest resistance. Specifically, a breakthrough itself is the forcible movement into a level not previously known. It is not like a gradual growth. You can have breakthroughs into new levels. Continual pushing can cause it, or you can break through instantaneously.

Breakthrough person. Someone who opens up a way in an area that has not previously been opened or gone into by any person associated with the breakthrough person.

Broken. Being in a particular position and realizing that it is not a proper position or posture. Rather than defending it, you become broken and contrite. Broken in this context is positive.

Brother. The natural definition is a male whom one is related to by birth, having the same father and mother. But in spiritual terminology, it is one who has the same father, God the Father.

B

Burden. Burden has both a positive and a negative connotation. In the negative, it means an oppressive weight or load that you might carry. But it can also refer to your having a burden for someone, which means that there is a continual pressure and weight upon you for the benefit of another; you could say, "I have a burden to preach in Russia." A burden is not self-oriented; it is an intercessory type of orientation.

Burnt offering. Something brought to the altar, set on fire, burnt, and totally consumed by fire in front of the person who brought it; the person could take nothing back. It is symbolic of worship. Worship and sacrifice are tied together in this respect. Worship is sacrifice because there is no personal benefit received. You can't bring a bullock and take cooked ribs home as the leftover. It is burnt entirely in front of you, and it is done for the act of doing it. Worship is a completed act in itself. The fact that you did it made it worship. It is not done to incur favor; it is done for God because He is God.

Calling. That which God has made known to you regarding what He wants you to do. You do not have to be called to preach; you can be called to do many things. Calling is God's making known to you what His divine will is for you to do in life. Anointing is the enablement that comes from receiving the call. There is no need for anointing until you understand your calling. However, there is a difference between gifts and calling. Your gifts are there to serve your calling. People may be gifted to sing, but they may be *called* to be worshippers. You are called to do what you are called to do, whether or not you ever do it. When you are gifted, God will never take His gifts back because they were not used right. You could take your gifts and make money but not necessarily ever fulfill your calling. There would then always be something a little special about what you do because God gifted you to do it, but it would not be an anointing; it would not lift burdens and destroy yokes. It would not be an anointing because it would not be going in the direction of your calling. Anointing has to do with the spiritual impact on people. (See Anointing; Anointing, law of; and Calling and confirmation.)

Calling and confirmation. Before a calling can be released, it requires confirmation. You can have a subjective understanding of your calling because a calling at some point has to be subjective. You have to know for yourself that you are called. But before your calling can be released, authority must confirm it.

C

Campmeeting. This term is used today to describe a large gathering of Christians who come to a series of meetings that generally have a variety of speakers and singers. The history of this term relates to the early days of revivals and the Spirit-filled movement in which people would actually meet at campgrounds and stay for weeks, sometimes months. Some people go to a particular place every year for a campmeeting. By comparison, crusades and revivals like those of Billy Sunday were a little more organized. They were not so informal. They had a specific purpose. They were at a particular city for a particular time, and then they moved on.

Captives. Those who are held in bondage.

Carnal. The state of being concerned with the lowest nature.

Cast out. A term used for the expelling of a demonic force out of a person. Binding is the prohibiting of the operation or the manifestation of the spirit. Casting out is the expelling of it. You cannot expel or cast out a spirit from people who do not want it cast out. There has to be an act of their will involved. But by your own authority you can bind it or keep it from operating. You can't cast it out of people if they are not willing to give it up, but you can bind it so that it does not operate in your presence. Binding does not always mean having to verbally say, "I bind that thing." Sometimes just the presence of your authority or something that you do will stop it.

Cell groups. Cell groups are small groups of Christians that belong to a larger body of Christians. They meet for fellowship, prayer, and instruction under the authority of headship. This works well in Dr. Cho's church, Yoido Full Gospel Church in South Korea, because he cannot seat all of his members in his church building. He has 750,000 members. So they meet and are pastored through delegated authority in their cell groups. A cell group can be somewhat evangelistic. The groups want to win people into the Body of Christ. There is an inherent danger with cell groups, though, in that they can become a breeding ground for false doctrine, rumors, and gossip, as well as be a drain on the host family. Also there is some concern about the decentralizing of authority and the downplaying of public gathering for corporate worship.

Cessation of charismas. This is the idea, held by some religious groups, that the gifts of the Spirit—especially anointings, miracles, and operations of the Spirit—stopped with the Apostles of the Lamb. Those who believe in the cessation of charismas do not believe that there are still apostles today. And they do not believe in the gifts, praying in tongues, or the gifts of healing and miracles.

Chaff. What the wind blows away from the wheat when it is being threshed into flour. It speaks to us of the unprofitable parts of our life, which get blown away from us whenever we are moving into a better position of being. (See Threshing floor.)

Chaos. The lack of order. (See Kingdom of chaos.)

C

Character. What God knows about you. It is the internal quality of being, who you are when no one else is watching. (See Reputation.)

Charismas. They are given not earned, and they are the same as gifts of the Spirit.

Charity. Used in the King James version of the Bible to mean love.

Chief shepherd. One of the titles given to Christ. Chief shepherd is Christ's distinction as the ultimate shepherd over all of the flock. Present day pastors are undershepherds.

Children's ministry. The many different organized fashions in which churches minister to their children.

Choice. A decision you make. We are all born with the ability to have choice. Choice means that God has given us the power of self-determination and that we are able to make decisions concerning our own well-being and our eternity. We are aided by a variety of things and hindered by a variety of things. But because we alone make the ultimate choice, we alone are ultimately responsible for the outcome.

Chosen. The elect of God.

Christ. A title of distinction given to Jesus.

Christ in you. Christ in you is the concept that the Anointed One, His anointing, and His characteristics are being lived out and released through you.

C

Christian. Followers of Christ who adhere to His principles.

Chronos and kairos. These are both delineations of time. *Chronos* means time, and *kairos* means timing. Chronos is where we get the word *chronometer*. It means the measure of time. It is the ticking of the clock. It is second-by-second, moment-by-moment. It never changes. It is set, permanent, and goes on and on. Kairos, on the other hand, has more to do with an understanding of season. It is not an exact demarcation of time, but rather it is a period of time that is identified by its purpose, not by the ticking of the clock. For example, you may have a calendar date that says this is when spring begins, which is the chronos, but the kairos, the actual season, is not subject to the clock or the calendar. So the weather may still act like it is winter for another six weeks because winter has a purpose. It is not bound by a date on the calendar. These words help us explain the seasons and timings of our lives. There is a time for some things, and there is a season for others.

Church. For something to truly be a church, it must have authority present. In other words, it is not just a gathering of peers. A fellowship and a Christian center are not the same as a church. For something to be a church, it must have authority. It must have structure. A church is the community of faith lived out. There is the universal church, and then there is the local church. The universal church includes followers of Christ who have been called out of darkness into the light. It is everybody who belongs to Jesus. Then there is the local, or individual, church. What Christ is to the church universal, the individual pastor is to the church local. Christ is the head of the universal church, and the pastor is the head of the local church. A church must have headship. It must have authority and structure, and it becomes the community of faith that people belong to after conversion. On the other hand, fellowship is peer level. Fellowship is two fellows in the same ship, peerage without authority. You can have fellowship without having a church, but you can't have a church without having fellowship.

Church age. The age or the demarcation of time at which the church is highlighted. It is the age of seeing God's kingdom on the earth.

Church, to have. To enjoy and to celebrate the presence of God.

Circumcision. There is, of course, the natural procedure, which is the removing of the foreskin. It is the actual flesh being cut away. But beyond that we have the spiritual concept of circumcision as a pastoral function. It symbolizes what happens when someone, especially someone in authority, takes the Word of God, which is also described as the sword of the Spirit, and through the proper use of the Word applied to our lives cuts away the excess flesh, baggage, and carnal attitudes of our lives. This is not always a pleasant experience. It is a painful, intense, and personal experience for someone to cut at our flesh. In the Old Testament, it was the right of a father. A father circumcised his son on the eighth day after birth, eight being the number of new beginnings. When you come to the New Testament, the Bible talks about circumcision of the heart. In other words, the flesh of the heart, the excess flesh and carnal baggage that you have carried, is cut away. This requires submission to the authority of another.

City church. Refers to all of the different individual believers and individual churches in a city as one entity. The term is used when all the Christians and churches in town are referred to as one.

Comfort. To comfort someone is to function in word or in deed in a way that lifts a burden and lessens struggles or pain.

Commandment. A decree or principled statement from God or a purposeful mandate from declared authority, both of which are void of option.

Committee. A group of people assigned to fulfill a particular task. It is an organization or a deployment, such as a committee on some particular thing. It oversees a particular task, handles the details of the task, and ultimately sees it to fruition.

Communicate. To communicate is to make thoughts, feelings, intentions, and understandings known to another person. Proper, full communication means that someone hears, receives, and understands what is said and is able to use it. Distorting truth and taking someone down a wrong path is using communication in a negative fashion. A general definition of communication is any method by which you convey a message to another person.

Communion. Comes from two words: common and union. Communion is spiritual interaction. Two or more

C

people in very close fellowship can be referred to as a communion. Communion is a two-way thing. It is also a word used to describe the Lord's Table.

Competition with authority. Can also be referred to as emulation. The word *emulation* means to try to be like someone else. But as it is used here, it implies a negative, envious state. When you see it in a church setting, emulation involves competition with authority. It involves people trying to outdo whoever is over them with the motivation of trying to replace them or being envious of a senior's position. Emulation is a continual competition with someone who is in authority.

Concert of Prayer. A concert of prayer is a large gathering of people—the entire church, for example—who pray at the same time. They do not necessarily pray the same thing, but they are praying in concert with one another.

Condemn. To judge someone negatively.

Condemnation. The act of judging someone negatively. Also the feeling of being judged and found to be wrong.

Conference. A conference is a large gathering of people. Generally, there is a registration fee. A conference usually has day sessions as well as evening sessions.

Confession. This doesn't mean telling sins to a priest. It actually comes from two words: *homo* and *lego*. It means to say the same thing. The principle of confession is that you are saying the same thing as God says about you, which is totally different from what Catholicism makes it. In born-again Christianity, your confession is what you say with faith out of your heart. Confession is also a specific statement of something. When you confess, you speak out of your heart, and you can have a positive or a negative confession. But it is whatever you speak that has faith attached to it. In other words, you can say "Man, I think I'm going to be sick. I think I'm going to die of cancer." Because you believe it, that's your confession. The words that come out of your mouth spring from your heart and have faith attached to them. Confession includes the idea that self-created truth is going to work for you or against you, depending upon whether it is self-created good or self-created bad.

Confidence. Confidence is self-assurance.

Confirmation. Confirmation is the recognition of something about someone by one of equal authority who does not know him or her or by one of a higher authority who recognizes and speaks externally to things that the person has believed are accurate. It is somewhat a Christian term. You may hear people say, "That's a confirmation to me." For example, three or four people are in a prayer group, and while they're praying about something, somebody says, "Well this is what I was thinking." If what that person was thinking happened to be what somebody else was thinking, one of the people may say, "That's a confirmation," because it validates what one of them was thinking. Most often in church settings these thoughts actually come from information that earlier went from one person to another. In other words, someone may have mentioned the thought earlier, but when it comes to someone in prayer or in some other way, it may feel to that person as if it is an external knowing. In reality, it was by virtue of comments that were heard earlier.

C

Here's another example. If I had been telling you for three weeks, "I'm really thinking about starting a business," and a week or two later I tell you about it again, I'm just throwing it out there. Then if one day when we are sitting around drinking coffee you tell me, "I had a dream last night that you had an antique business," I may think, "That's a confirmation." People do this all the time, but it's *not* confirmation.

For true confirmation to come on the peer level, it has to come from someone who has *no* knowledge at all of any of the facts involved. For example, let's say that you ran into someone at the grocery store who didn't know your state of affairs, and that person said, "I was praying about you the other day, and I had this dream that I saw you surrounded by a bunch of antiques." Now *that* may be a genuine confirmation.

Confirmation can also come from someone outside your peer level. For confirmation to come this way, it has to come from headship ministry. For example, a person is not a prophet until the *prophets* say that person is a prophet. Positions, such as that of prophet, in the church are held by those who have been confirmed in that office. Confirmation may come to the individual, but the individual's place in the ministry should also be recognized by those to whom he or she ministers. For examples, if someone sings a song on the platform in church and does really well, people should encourage that person and tell him or her that it was wonderful. But it would be wrong for a member of the congregation or for someone outside the church to say, "I think you need to be making religious records. I think you need to get on the road." The proper headship ministry has not confirmed that. Even if people have a desire to be on the praise team, to have records, or to be on the road, they are supposed to hold onto that until those who are in authority say, "I think it is time for you to get on the praise team; I think it is time for you to make records." *That* is confirmation. People who feel they have something need to have it confirmed by authority. This is the principle of understanding confirmation. Confirmation comes from those of higher authority. God the Father confirmed Jesus because there was nobody on earth who outranked him. When Jesus was baptized, a voice from heaven said, "This is my Son in whom I am well pleased." God the Father confirmed Jesus. When Jesus healed the lepers, He told them to show themselves to the priests because they could not be considered clean until the priests confirmed it. (See Calling and Authority.)

Conflict. Warring positions. Conflict demands at least two parties. One can be at odds with the other or even persecute the other. Once they enter into it, it becomes conflict. Conflict comes from positions or opinions that are actively striving for dominance.

Congregation. Used to describe everyone who is sitting in a church at any given time. It does not necessarily mean only those who are members of the church. If you show up at somebody's church on Sunday, you are part of that congregation.

Conscience. Your internal voice regarding what is right and wrong.

Consecrated. Something that is set apart for God's use.

C

Contention. More than one person in active opposition. Contention has to have the involvement of both parties. Having an adversary does not necessitate fighting. Someone can be your adversary without your becoming involved in actual opposition or struggle with him or her. However, if you do enter into a struggle against your adversary, then you are in contention.

Conversion. Conversion refers to the process of repenting and being born again. It involves the process of going from one direction to another direction. To convert is to change over, to change positions.

Conviction. The discernible feeling of God's dealing with unbelievers, drawing them into repentance. The feeling could make unbelievers think to themselves, "As soon as the preacher gets done, I need to run up there and get saved. I'm out of relationship with God." That feeling is called conviction. It does not necessarily bring a person into an understanding of God. It is the feeling that God is dealing with you about repentance or wrong. It is a basic, fundamental first step. People have to be aware that God is dealing with them before they can be dealt with.

Believers can also be convicted of a particular action, attitude, or manner of life. Conviction can also be defined as the deep-rooted feeling and passion by which one communicates; a person can preach with conviction, or someone can sing with conviction. In a spiritual context, people usually can't demonstrate conviction unless they really have it. If you have conviction though, you can provoke it in others and cause them to be convicted. When Peter preached on the day of Pentecost, those who

C

were listening were pricked in their hearts. His message got through to them, and they were convicted.

Cornerstone. The stone set in the corner of the building; the squaring and alignment of the building are based on this stone. It lies on top of or is a part of the foundation. In the metaphorical sense, Jesus is the cornerstone. He is a part of the foundation by which everything else takes its bearings.

Corporate anointing. Corporate anointing is the discernible atmosphere, presence, and empowerment of people who flow and work together under spiritual authority and unity and produce a particular grace and atmosphere in which they then function.

Counsel. Counsel is receiving input and advice in a particular area, especially from someone who has knowledge and wisdom.

Countenance. In the physical sense, countenance is the entire expression of the face. But it also is the reflection of the inner man through the expression of the face.

Counterfeit. Anything false whose purpose is to misrepresent itself as something that is authentic.

Covenant. A legal and binding agreement. It goes beyond a meeting of the minds. It is an agreement entered into by more than one person, and all that each person is and possesses becomes at the availability of anyone else in covenant. A covenant is a special relationship. Sometimes this word is used too loosely; a covenant is an agreement of a deep and total nature. We

C

are in covenant with God, and that covenant was incurred by the shedding of Christ's blood. His blood purchased for us everything that God has. When you come into covenant with God through Christ, everything that God has is now working for you.

Cover. To watch over, to guard, to guide, and to protect; to oversee.

Covering. The spiritual function of the foregoing word. Covering is the space and the scope to which the guiding, protecting, and leading are extended. In a spiritual sense, it is like being under the covering of a tent or the covering of an umbrella. (See Authority.)

Create. To bring into being out of nothingness.

Cross. The cross and the crucifixion are the significant points against which things have to be measured. For example, some things come to the cross and die because they are fulfilled. Some things come to the cross and go from the natural to the spiritual. Some things pass through the cross and remain unchanged. For example, the feasts, ordinances, and dietary laws come to the cross and die because they are fulfilled. Jesus said, "I did not come to destroy the law; I came to fulfill it." Circumcision, for example, goes from a natural ordinance and into a spiritual understanding as it passes through the cross. Things such as David's writings on praising the Lord pass through the cross unchanged. When I say "pass through the cross," I do not mean that something passes through a physical tree. The phrase implies the significance of and the changing of events at the crucifixion. The cross is also known in scriptural terminology as the *Tree* and has a reference to both Adam and Christ. Adam took of one tree. Christ was hung on the wood of another tree. Adam partook of the fruit of one tree, and Christ became the fruit of the other tree.

Crowns. A distinction of royalty, authority, and victory.

Crucified. A form of death. There is a spiritual aspect to this as well. Paul said, "I crucify the flesh daily." In other words, he spiritually crucified the corporal body that would war against the Spirit. "I crucify it daily" means "I put it to death." He did not literally mean nailing his flesh, but he reminded himself, "I am alive in the Spirit, and I count myself as being crucified with Christ." Crucifixion is the concept of your looking to deny or to remove yourself from the flesh world and to concentrate more heavily on the spiritual realm. The flesh has certain appetites, desires, boundaries, and restrictions. Metaphorically speaking, crucifying or denying the flesh accentuates spiritual understanding.

Crucifix. A crucifix is a cross with a depiction of Christ on it.

Curse. Somebody's creating or attempting to create for somebody else a negative affliction. It is also a negative spiritual force that works to hold people in bondage, that robs them of peace and tranquillity, and that thwarts them from the enjoyment of their total potential. (See Damned.)

Damned. Damned is not just the idea of someone's saying, "You're damned, and you're going to hell." A person has to accept it, and then he or she is damned. When people accept the condemnation or the curse from whatever source it came and take it unto themselves, then they are damned because of it. You could say the words to curse someone, but the words do not mean that the person has been damned. To curse is to intend to cause harm and negative outcome in someone. Damned, on the other hand, is someone's acceptance of the outcome of having been cursed. (See Curse.)

Dance. As it relates to Christianity, it is one of the ways to give honor and praise to God. In this context, it is a spontaneous response to God's favor, victory, deliverance, physical healing, and salvation.

Dark Ages. An historical period of time. It was called the Dark Ages due to the lack of inventions and the lack of the illumination of the Holy Spirit. It occurred when Roman Catholicism and religiosity dominated the world. The Dark Ages are referred to as spiritually dark because the windows of heaven were closed. Salvation through the acceptance of Christ had been done away with, and people were supposed to be saved through receiving the sacraments of a church. Catholicism had established the infallibility of the Pope, infant baptism, and things of this nature. Bibles were taken out of the hands of the people. There was no illumination or spiritual light.

D

The Reformation of 1517 took place when Martin Luther received illumination on the scriptures, when he realized that the just shall live by faith, not by works of righteousness, and that no man is justified by works but only by faith. When Luther got that, a very large uproar began. Finally, in protest, from which the word "Protestant" comes, he wrote ninety-five theses about the seven indulgences, the infallibility of the Pope, and the taking of Bibles out of the hands of the people. But primarily Luther was concerned with the *priesthood of all believers*, which means that all believers have direct access to God. Luther took these ideas to the Wittenberg Cathedral and nailed them on the door as a sign of protest. That action began the Protestant Reformation. Next came Guttenberg and his printing press. Guttenberg started putting Bibles back into the hands of the people. When people started getting light and illumination, they found that Catholicism and these other things were not at all what Jesus had said. The beginning of the Renaissance followed the Dark Ages. (See Reformation.)

Darkness. The absence of light, and light here refers to understanding and illumination. Darkness is blindness. It is being surrounded by evil or by the absence of understanding.

Deacon. In the local church, a position that comes from the word *deaconian*, which means to serve. Deacons are generally in charge of practical and physical matters of the church or of the ministry. In many churches, there are both elders and deacons; elders are usually in charge of spiritual matters, and deacons are in charge of practical matters. Sometimes deacons are in charge of things like hospital visitations. In other churches, deacons are in charge of building programs and so forth. They have varying areas of responsibility. They are not usually involved in doctrine, spiritual welfare, handling disciplinary problems, finances, or other things of that nature.

Dead. Dead is sometimes used as a term that refers to something that is non-operative, cold, or non-responsive. A church can be dead if there is no life of the Holy Spirit functioning. Dead can also mean to be shut off to something, exemplified by the phrase "dead to sin." (See Death.)

Deaf and dumb spirit. Every person who is unable to speak or hear does not necessarily have a deaf and dumb spirit. But there are spirits that can cause physical manifestations. There is more than one spirit of infirmity, and the spirit of deaf and dumb is one of them. Deafness and dumbness are the manifestation such a spirit would cause, and when it is cast out, a person can speak and hear.

Deafness. In the natural sense, deafness is the inability to hear and perceive auditory sounds. In the spiritual sense, deafness refers to someone who is not hearing and understanding or who is refusing to hear what God is saying.

Death. There are three aspects of death. The first aspect is the cessation of biological function. It takes place when the body quits working. The second aspect is to consider yourself separated from something. For example, "I am alive unto righteousness but dead unto sin." To be separated from something and from its effect is to

D

be dead to it. People can be dead unto God. The third aspect of death is *eternal* separation from God. That's why the term "born again" is used. Before people are born again, they are dead unto God. They are separated from God. Therefore, when they become saved, they are reborn and made alive unto God.

Deceived. To be deceived is to accept illusion and falsehood as truth and to begin to operate with them.

Decently and in order. This phrase refers to a principle and process. It involves the principles upon which you build your life and the subsequent process of ordering those principles. The process is deciding what comes first and what follows. It is the proper position and principles upon which your life is based, and it includes the motivations and methods by which you live. If you have the proper motivation and the proper principles, you do things in the proper order and with the proper methods. That is decently and in order. It necessarily follows from headship and authority.

Deception. Something that appears to be real but is built on falsehood and illusion.

Decree. A statement of purpose; a setting of something into motion that carries authority with it.

Defeat. The position of having accepted that you are conquered.

Defeated spirit. A person has a defeated spirit when he or she has given up before the battle, opposition, or opportunity has presented itself. There are a lot of peo-

D

ple with defeated spirits. It can become a corporate term when it affects a whole faction of people. For example, high schools and societies that decide to give out clean needles to drug addicts have a defeated spirit. They have already admitted defeat. They feel that they cannot fix or change the situation. Therefore, they feel overcome and defeated by it and give up. (See Wounded spirit.)

Deliverance. Deliverance is pulling a person from beneath bondage or demonic control.

Demand on the anointing. It is sometimes referred to as *placing a demand on the anointing* or *pulling on the anointing.* It takes place when those to whom the ministry and anointing is coming increase its effectiveness by recognizing it and facilitating it in their life. In other words, it is not passive. The learner is as active as the teacher is. The recipient of the gift is as active as the giver of the gift. For example, if a person preaches at a church at which everyone just sits and looks at him or her, then there is not much demand placed on his or her anointing. But if the people begin to respond and to pull or to place a demand on that anointing, then his anointing will rise to another level. It can be very interesting. People can preach at a church and know more about a subject than they are able to share because there is no demand. Like the law of supply and demand, if there is no demand, there is going to be no supply. There is no demand when the listeners are not doing anything with what is taught and when they don't really seem to care much about it. In other instances, a person may know information, but the demand of the listeners on the anointing is so strong that he or she starts understanding things not known before standing up to speak. God

D

starts pushing new information through the speaker because the people are continuing to pull on the anointing.

Demons. Created beings whose origin was in a class of angels. Demons are fallen angels. One-third of the angels fell with Lucifer when he was cast out of heaven. Demons are of unspecified number and do the bidding of Satan. They work against God, good, light, and His creation.

Denominational spirit. A mentality and disposition that comes with those who are part of any sect or denomination. They put the well-being, furthering, and self-preservation of the denomination at pre-eminence in their life, even beyond what God may be currently doing in the earth.

Destiny. The place of arrival and fulfillment for which a person was born.

Destroyer. A name or designation given to the Devil.

Devil. Lucifer or Satan. With a small-case "d," the devil is interchangeable for demon. You can say that a person has an unclean demon or an unclean devil; a person can be possessed by a demon or possessed by a devil. Being possessed by the Devil is being possessed by Lucifer through a chain of authority. God is omnipresent. The Devil is not. Therefore, he must possess someone through a chain of authority.

Devourer. Also a name or distinction given to the Devil. This name refers to his eating a person's resources, energies, and potential. This aspect of the Devil is sometimes likened to a plague of locusts.

Diligence. The spiritual dynamic of consistently and earnestly seeking to do what you know to do. Persisting to do good.

Discerning of spirits. To discern spirits is to internally know or to pick up on whether or not what you are dealing with is a spirit. Discerning of spirits is also the understanding or internal knowing of what spirit you are dealing with. Somebody who is having a bad day is not necessarily stuck with the spirit of something; the person may simply be having a bad day. A spirit is an entity and a force that is doing something and that is outside of oneself and not from one's own origin. A danger for Christians is thinking that everything may be a spirit. For example, if a person goes outside and doesn't have a coat on, he or she may get wet, start sneezing, and then think that a spirit of infirmity has attacked. That's not a spirit. And you don't have a *bill* demon when you have overcharged your credit cards. Everybody's having a bad day is not the spirit of anger. Discerning of spirits is being able to determine whether or not what you are dealing with is actually a spirit.

Discernment. Discernment is the ability to internally know something. To discern means to know. Discernment is not the ignoring of natural data or information. More often it is the proper assimilation of it. Some people think that discernment means that there can be no natural input at all. Discernment is definitely on a spiritual level, but it does not mean that there are not natural indicators that draw one's attention to some-

D

thing. Discernment is seeing the bigger picture or the broader context in something that may be natural or of the soul. Sometimes when you see something natural, it is a sign that is indicative of a larger picture.

Disciple. One who follows and who is developing in the discipline of what he or she is being taught.

Discipline. A corrective action to bring about positive change. For example, we use discipline for children. It also is the state of being in charge of your emotions, physically and spiritually, instead of having them be in charge of you. It also defines an area of interest in education. Math is a discipline. It means to align, to discipline something into line as a corrective influence.

Disconnect. To disconnect is to separate from a person or a situation. Occasionally, it can be a negative thing when someone disconnects from a person or situation that was very positive. But essentially, disconnection is the action or the circumstance of having removed oneself from a suppressive influence. This is not always just a matter of physical proximity. It has to do with the realm of the spirit and of the soul. For example, you could work with someone, and although you must remain on the job, you may feel a need to disconnect from the person's soul because the person has a bad attitude in general. To disconnect means to no longer allow someone else's emotions to have a bearing on your emotions. To disconnect is to refuse to be joined and aligned with something or with someone else's soul or spirit. Sometimes disconnection requires a physical separation as well.

Disobedience. Disobedience is willfully acting against known truth.

Diverse tongues. There are two meanings. Diverse tongues is the manifestation of speaking in tongues or in the Spirit. It is a language given to the believer by the Holy Spirit that is not learned and is not of earthly origin. It also includes the ability to speak in an earthly language that you were never taught, which would be a sign and a wonder. Every person has a prayer language and a way that they pray in the Spirit. But there are also times, especially in intercessory prayer, when a diverse tongue may come upon you. For example, you could be in an intercession group, praying for the mission team in Africa, when all of a sudden your tongue may have a whole different dynamic to it. It may be a different tongue than what you normally use. It may have a decidedly African quality to it. That would be a manifestation of diverse tongues.

Diversity and unity. Diversity and unity is the concept that there can be diversity in the midst of unity because unity is not sameness. The Bible uses the body analogy, which describes how we are members of the same body but have different purposes and functions. The eyes serve a different purpose than the hands do. But there is unity in the body despite all of its diverse members and parts. Unity is not conformity. Unity incorporates diversity under headship and authority and moves for the same purposes.

Divorce. *Di* means two, and *vorce* means way. It means to go two ways. It means to separate from the covenant.

D

Doctrine. Foundational truths. A set group of principles or beliefs that other truths are built upon. These teachings are fundamental to any group, belief, or church.

Doctrine of devils. Includes philosophies, teachings, or theologies that build up a rationale in people's minds that keeps them from the truth.

Dominion. Taking authority or exercising authority. Dominion applies to God and man, but it also applies to Satan. Where is your dominion? Dominion is only wherever you exercise it. It means taking authority.

Don't curse your crisis. This is the concept that crisis is the nature of change. Crisis can be an indication that you have outgrown the previous level you were in. Most of us are taught throughout our life to avoid, to alleviate, and to run from anything that causes pain or crisis. But you can see in Scripture and in your life that many times a crisis reveals your internal strength, which you did not know you possessed. A crisis can help you to identify who your true friends are, as well as who your enemies are. It can become the fuel for your own personal revival and the bridge that takes you to the next dimension of your life.

Double portion. Having what your progenitor gave you and what you add to it. The double portion ultimately means that you begin where someone else ended. In the natural sense, the double portion belongs by birthright to the first-born, who receives the land of the estate. Double portion is the understanding that you now begin your life in the place at which the other person ended;

D

you start with that person's portion and add your own. (See Birthright.)

Doubt. To be unsure.

Dreams. Dreams in the natural sense are one of the ways that God speaks to people. They are the dramas played out in the mind. But the spiritual connotation is the ability to envision something, to hope for it, and to be positively directed toward it even when it is not yet reality.

Dry. To be without moisture. Dry speaks of being stale. The Holy Spirit is often referred to as water, rain, or oil, and to be dry is to have a lack of the Holy Spirit.

Earth. The planet on which we live. Metaphorically speaking, man is made from the earth. The Bible says we have a treasure in earthen vessels. Our body is made from the earth, and there are comparisons between the earth and man.

Ecclesia. Called-out ones. The term is equal to the English word *church*. If you look at the word *church* in Greek, it is *ekklesia*.

Ecclesiastical. The things that pertain to church structure and organization in general.

Edify. To build up. To make strong.

Egypt. Metaphorically represents bondage and a life of sin.

Elder. It can be someone who is older. It is also a person who outranks you spiritually, a person who has a greater measure of spiritual authority. Also, it is a function and position held in the church that carries with it spiritual authority and responsibility.

Emulation. (See Competition with authority.)

End-time theology. (See Eschatology.)

E

End times. The span of time in human development just before the second coming of Christ to earth. It is without particular demarcation.

Enemy. With a capital "E," it is another name given to Satan or Lucifer. With a lower case "e," it is a person who purposely and actively takes a position against you to do you harm.

Engage. To initiate and pursue conflict in spiritual warfare.

Enlightenment. In the spiritual sense, it is the position of being able to see things from a clear, unbiased perspective. To have your consciousness lifted by hearing the Word of God and being in fellowship with people. By reading the Word of God, you can also come into enlightenment on a particular subject matter. There can be enlightenment in given areas such as Scripture. Enlightenment is an understanding of God. The origin of enlightenment is external, meaning that it comes from outside of you. Something enlightens you. It can be a word, an action, or a deed, but it can also be something spiritual. It is something you comprehend, and that comprehension brings you into a greater understanding of God.

Envy. The negative state of being that results from an inordinate ill feeling about someone else's place, material gain, or success. Envy is the inordinate desire to have what is someone else's in place, prestige, or possessions. Covetousness is somewhat different because it is usually associated with the property of another person. For example, "Thou shalt not covet thy neighbor's wife." Or, for example, if you have a Mercedes that I really want, if I want *your* Mercedes, that's coveting. Envy, on the other hand, is thinking that because I don't have a Mercedes, I don't want *you* or anyone else to have one. Envy is the ill feeling toward someone due to something he or she has. It is thinking that other people do not deserve what they have but somehow you do.

Equipping. A spiritual function by which one person enables and empowers another person to perform a certain task. Ephesians 4 says that the apostle, prophet, pastor, evangelist, and teacher are called to equip the saints. Equipping implies training. It is the process by which believers are trained and empowered to function in spiritual principles and to come into maturity.

Eros. Love, as in sensual, sexual love. (See Love.)

Eschatology. The study of the end times. (See Rapture.)

Establish. Notice the word *stable* in the middle of it. It means to bring something into a position of stability or permanency so that other things can be built upon it. What is being built comes out of speculation into being known and understood.

Eternal life. Eternal life is eternity in the presence of God, as opposed to eternal death, which is eternal separation from God's presence.

Evangelist. A person who carries the good news, especially to those who are not converted.

Exalt. Exalt means to lift high and to magnify.

E

Excellence. The quality of spirit and nature manifested in the performance of tasks when a person completes them with quality to the best of his or her ability.

Expository. Expository describes the teaching of the Bible line-upon-line and verse-by-verse. Some preachers may start in the book of John go verse-by-verse, chapter-by-chapter, through the whole book.

External. Refers to all things outside the body.

Extol. To bestow. It is an old English word for exalt. It is a conveying of exaltation.

Extra-biblical. Something that is not found in Scripture but may be used in practical religion.

Faith. Faith is a deep conviction of internal belief that produces corresponding action. Faith works from the inside out, not the outside in. Faith is based on a promise, not a problem. Faith causes you to prioritize things. Faith gives you a different perspective because faith is not based on things that are tangible or discernible through only natural circumstances. Faith is also the inward knowing and complete assurance of something for which there is no corporal or material evidence. (See Gift of faith.)

Faithfulness. In the Christian context, it is the quality of being consistent, proven over a given period of time, which makes a person trustworthy, loyal, and true to a set of ethical or moral principles. It requires a period of continuous time and a continuing adherence to an ethical standard. It is a state of being that implies consistency.

Fall. Fall implies a downward motion from one state or position into a lower state or position. Satan fell from his first mistake. When Adam transgressed, that was the fall of Adam.

Falling under the power of God. Sometimes referred to as falling out. It is also sometimes referred to as being slain in the Spirit, but this may be a poor use of terms; if you were ever slain in the Spirit, you wouldn't get back up. If you were slain, you'd be killed. Falling under the power of God is a physical reaction to a spiritual impact.

F

At certain times when the Holy Spirit is dealing directly with the spirit of man, the spiritual reality overrides the natural reality, and therefore, the body is temporarily out of commission. This occurs as a result of the Holy Spirit. The body falls because it is not used to this and is not involved in this. As we function in the material world, the physical body is in charge of our movements; however, on the occasions when the Holy Spirit is dealing directly with our spirit and is bypassing the physical body's involvement, the body is out of commission and is suspended or attenuated. This is not a loss of consciousness. It is not being in a coma. It is not passing out. It is the Holy Spirit's dealing directly with the human spirit.

False doctrine. A belief system or code of principles that people accept as truth and that generally involve scriptures that have been twisted.

False prophet. A person who prophesies falsely. What they say does not come to pass, or they prophesy for the wrong motivation, purpose, or intent.

False witness. People who say they saw something or know something that they, in fact, do not are false witnesses. This is somewhat different from lying. A false witness brings harm to another person in a different way than lying would. Specifically, a false witness says something against another person that is not true and that harms that person.

Familiar spirits. A classification of spirits; these spirits pose as people who are dead and try to bring people into the dark side of spiritual realities. To pull this off, they have to be familiar with both the person who is deceased and the person who is alive. The familiar spirit is essentially inhuman and has never had a body; it is a fallen angel or a demon.

Famine. Famine is a term we use to describe the place of those who are without the nourishment of the Word of God.

Fasting. Fasting generally refers to food. It is the act of putting away food and replacing it with times of prayer. It is not just asceticism. It is part of disciplining the body and reminding the body that it is not in charge. It also does not just mean putting away food because you can put away food and not replace it with prayer. Prayer should always accompany fasting.

Fear of the Lord. The fear of the Lord is the beginning of wisdom. And through the fear of the Lord, men depart from evil. It is maintaining great respect and honor for God as the authority. It does not imply fear but rather awe and reverence.

Feed. To feed is to nourish someone else's mind, heart, and spirit through the teaching of the Word.

Fellowship. Fellowship is interacting with peers on a soul level, which produces the exchange of ideas, thoughts, and feelings on a kind and benevolent, not overly impacting, level. Spirituality is not fellowship; that would be communion. Fellowship is on a soul level. (See Communion and Church.)

F

Fig tree. There is the natural fig tree. But a fig tree is also a representation or word picture of religiosity. It goes back to Adam. Adam sinned and made a covering for himself of fig leaves. So Jesus, in Mark 11, cursed the fig tree and said, "No man will eat fruit of you from this day forward." The fig tree then is a type, shadow, word picture, or symbol of the religious system by which men seek to cover their own sinfulness. This system does not have the fruit of spiritual realities or understandings.

Fire. Actually, the word *zeal* parallels the word *fire*. It means to be consumed with and to burn with great passion for something.

First fruit. A term that describes the tithe. It speaks of giving to God what is first, what is the best. It is the position of the first of your increase.

Five-fold ministry. The five-fold ministry includes the apostle, prophet, pastor, evangelist, and teacher. The apostle lays foundation, establishes people, and brings revelation and understanding. The prophet tells us the direction we are going and what he or she hears at the present time. People with teaching gifts say, "Okay, now this is what the apostle said, and here's how this works." And they begin to break it down systematically. The pastors have concern and care; they have an ongoing care and concern for a local assembly. They are referred to sometimes as married to the church. They comfort the churchgoers, correct them, feed them, and lead them. They are with them in season and out of season. They help to make the church into a family. The evangelist has the special ministering gift that pulls people toward conversion. All of these can be offices or ministry gifts, but they also all have particular anointings.

Flesh. Flesh is a term that designates the lower nature of man, the carnal nature that is ruled by basic lusts and desires and that includes things like envy. It includes basal characteristics.

Flesh and blood. Refers to something originated of man. It may encompass the mind, the imagination, or the heart of man, but it is not divine in nature. Flesh and blood refers to something that is human in nature.

Flock. A term used to describe a particular gathering of believers.

Flow. A discernible movement and direction of the Spirit of God. When entered into, a person's energies are enhanced by going with the flow and moving in the same direction, instead of swimming upstream and fighting it.

Follow. To make someone else's direction your direction.

Follow-up. Used to describe a church ministry in which new converts receive personal attention and correspondence to encourage them to continue in the faith.

Following. The process of doing the above. It could also be used to describe a group of people who ascribe to a similar belief system and personal leader.

Fool. A person who shuns knowledge, despises correction, and continuously blunders in life.

F

Forgive. Not holding against someone's account wrong that has been done. You forgive yourself as well as others.

Forgiveness. The act of being released from the punitive thoughts, feelings, or actions of someone; you can be released by another person, yourself, or God.

Former rain. Spiritual renewals that predate the twentieth century are referred to as the former rain. There was a movement right after the turn of the twentieth century that was referred to as the latter rain movement.

Fornication. Sex outside of marriage. (See Adultery.)

Fortify. The act of preparing and strengthening something.

Forward untangling. People of greater authority should be free from entanglements of lower things so that they can give their attention to higher and greater things, which can affect more people for the positive. For example, Acts 5 says that the Grecian widows and the Jewish widows did not feel as if they were being treated the same. They came to the apostles and said, "You need to do something about this." The apostles said, "You look out amongst yourselves and take care of this. We should not leave the Word of God and prayer to wait on tables." People of greater authority, whose words and deeds affect the greatest number of people at the greatest speed, should not be wasting their faith, their attention, their energy, and their resources dealing with who has what in their soup. Let the person making the soup do that.

I use the term *forward untangling* to refer to untangling those who forward the faith, those who are leading. We untangle them so that everything can more easily move forward. Forward untangling is doing whatever you can to assist those in senior positions so that they can better direct the church body. Once you are in agreement with the aims and goals of people in authority over you, realize that the easier you make life for them, the better they can steer the boat and direct everyone on board. If you are *not* seeking to ease the load of people above you, you are indicating that you have resentment toward or disagreement with them. It's an easy test to determine who is on board and who isn't. Identify who is helping and who is criticizing, who is untangling the forward motion and who isn't. The concept of forward untangling can be applied in many areas. Forward untangling is making sure that whoever is pulling or steering or guiding is free from encumbrances so that everything can be moved unhindered. (See Measure of authority and Ministry of helps.)

Foundation. The rudimentary, basic elements on which something is built.

Freedom. Freedom is the state of being that involves the lack of negative constraints or bondage. It does not necessarily involve all areas of life at one time. You can be free in one area and be bound in another. A person comes into freedom when he or she has a lack of imposed constraints. Freedom is not the total lack of any restraint, however. It is the lack of the negative. It is a state of being in which you don't have negative bondage or restraints imposed upon you. Being free brings you into the position at which the question becomes what you are free from and what you are free to do. When you are free to have the power of self-determination, you are free to make choices. You are free to do other things. You are not free to do whatever you wish, however.

Fresh anointing. Fresh anointing is being re-invigorated and re-energized by the Holy Spirit; it involves newness and something not done before.

Fresh oil. A similar concept to fresh anointing. Oil is symbolic of being anointed.

Fruit. The end result of an action, thought, or intent. The harvest of seed sown.

Fruit of the Spirit. The fruit of the Spirit can be distinguished from the gifts of the Spirit. Gifts are given. Fruit is grown and matured. It takes time. For example, there is no gift of patience, gift of love, gift of longsuffering, or gift of gentleness. These are things that you have to grow and develop. Nine is the number of fruitfulness in the Scripture because there are nine fruits of the Spirit, nine gifts of the Spirit, and nine months before a woman gives birth. The nine fruits of the Spirit are love, joy, peace, patience, kindness, goodness, faithfulness, gentleness, and self-control.

Frustration. A fear-based emotion. Frustration is a result of being uncoordinated with the season in which God has you. It is being uncoordinated with the will of God. It is also the fear that your efforts will not pay off.

Fulfill. To be filled full. It means for something to have come to its point of fruition.

Gabriel. An archangel. (See Archangel.)

Garden of Eden. Where God placed Adam and Eve.

Garment. Clothing. In the metaphoric sense, it refers to a variety of things with which you can clothe yourself mentally and spiritually. The Bible says that God has given you a garment of praise for the spirit of heaviness. You replace the spirit of heaviness by wearing the garment of praise. A garment is the attitude, the spirit of, and the essence of. Garments are symbolic of and metaphoric of attitudes, spirits, and dispositions.

Gentile. In the light of the New Covenant, it refers to people who are unbelievers or are outside of the Covenant. In the Old Testament, it referred to somebody who wasn't Jewish.

Gentleness. One of the fruits of the Spirit. The ability to interact without causing disruption, concern, or alarm. To be calming, non-abrasive, and polite.

Get off my boat. The phrase "get off my boat" comes from the story of Jonah and the whale. There was smooth sailing on the boat headed to Nineveh until Jonah got on. And then there was a storm until the people on the boat finally realized that Jonah was the cause of their trouble. So they threw him off of the boat, and the whale swallowed him.

G

Get off my boat is the principle that if someone with internal conflicts enters your circle of influence, those conflicts will be produced externally. At some point, you will find that the storms and difficulties and problems you have are a result of the person who came into your world and produced the storm. The only way for you to deal with this, however long it takes you to come to realize it, is to push them off your boat and outside your circle of influence. Frequently we go through a process by which we feel that we can fix these people or that we can help them. Sooner or later, when you get tired of the storm and everything else, you realize that you can't. The storms will not quit because the person is out of the will of God. The person is living contrary to his or her environment. He or she has internal issues that haven't been told. The only way that you can help people like this is to throw them off and let God send a fish to swallow them up and take them where they are supposed to go. It is better to do that than to allow them to sink your own boat while you fruitlessly try to help them.

Gift of. Denotes special ability, grace, and empowerment given by the Holy Spirit to aid believers in effecting God's will.

Gift of discerning of spirits. First, lets a person know whether something's origin is human personality (a natural occurrence) or spirit in nature. It may subsequently then make a person aware of whether the spirit is of God or not. And if not, in many cases it will make a person aware of the origin and intent of the evil spirit.

Gift of faith. A manifestation of one of the nine gifts of the Holy Spirit. A gift denotes that it is not earned, merited, or orchestrated by the will of man. When the gift of faith is in operation, a person has a supernatural ability to believe, and it is nearly impossible not to believe. The Holy Spirit initiates this in the life of a believer for a specific time, place, purpose, or season. It is not a state in which people generally stay for a great period of time, but it exists to bring miracle power to people in need, in spite of their own lack or ability to believe in the face of contradictory evidence. Doubt and unbelief have no bearing when the gift of faith is operating.

Gift of interpretation of tongues. Grants a person the ability to understand or interpret what that person or another has vocalized in tongues. The mystery is revealed. We are admonished to pray with the Spirit and with understanding also.

Gift of prophecy. It is of slightly higher order than tongues and interpretation. It reveals the will, intent, or mind of God to people. It involves edification, exhortation, and comfort. On its highest level, it becomes creative and can set into motion God's will.

Gift of the word of knowledge. Is the understanding or knowledge of something a person would not know by natural means. It is internal knowledge.

Gift of the word of wisdom. A divine answer or solution. Knowing what to do, even in an area that a person has no experience in.

Gift of the working of miracles. A special grace that produces awe and wonderment in those who witness something impossible being done through the individual with this gift operating. Many times something natural is used to set into motion the working of miracles. For example, Samson killed a thousand Philistines with the jawbone of an ass. Moses used his shepherd's rod to bring water from a rock, and Jesus put clay in a man's eyes to restore sight. Something must be done to ignite the miracle; this gives an act the distinction of being the working of miracles.

Gift of tongues. Praying in the language of the Spirit. It is not an earthly language or one that is learned. Diverse tongues can cause a person to speak in an earthly dialect not learned. When a person prays or speaks in tongues, he or she is speaking things that are mysteries hidden from natural thought.

Gift of wisdom. The gift of wisdom is the ability to rightfully decide, determine, and know what to do, even in areas you have no previous experience in or knowledge of. It is a gift of the Holy Spirit.

Gifts. Given by God; they are not earned. A person can develop in a lot of areas, one of which is the area of gifts. Music, for example, is a gift. A person who has no musical gift can study music and still not quite get it. God gives gifts as He wills to enable people to fulfill their calling, and the gifts and callings of God are without repentance. God will not take them back. He will not revoke them if you don't use them properly.

Gifts of healing. Operates to bring blessing to the sick, diseased, and infirm. A special empowerment of the Holy Spirit given to individuals by which they have the capacity to be extremely effective in bringing healing to the

G

sick. In its greatest measure, it is not the recipient's faith that is at issue but rather the blessing imparted by the possession of the gift.

Gifts of the Spirit. The gifts of the Holy Spirit are divine in nature. They are supernatural abilities, *charismas*, or graces given to God's people. It is important to note that although they are available for all Spirit-filled believers, they do not operate on command or at the behest of individuals. A person should be open, willing, and yielded to God's purposes, knowing that He is the giver of the gifts that serve as signs and wonders to humanity. The nine gifts of the Spirit can be classified as follows:
• Three vocal gifts: Tongues, Interpretation of Tongues, and Prophecy
• Three power gifts: Healing, Faith, and the Working of Miracles
• Three revelation gifts: Word of Wisdom, Word of Knowledge, and Discerning of Spirits
These gifts of the Holy Spirit give the believer a great advantage in the world and over the adversary. Although they are gifts, a person can learn over time to be more sensitive to them and to be more accurate and proper in the administration of them.

Glory. The manifest presence of God. God is everywhere at all times, but He is not manifested everywhere at all times. Manifest means that you can feel and sense it. Glory is the heaviness of the presence of God, which does not mean sadness but means that a person has awareness that God is not to be taken lightly.

Goats. We sometimes refer to those in the church as sheep. In addition to sheep, though, there also are goats, which are similar to sheep but are stubborn and resistant. They eat anything, and they are always butting up against something. They are amongst the sheepfold, but they are always making that noise that drives you crazy. They are independent and frequently have a nasty disposition. Also, goats do things that sheep won't do. Goats, when they are done drinking out of a brook, for example, will defecate in it. Sheep won't do that. Metaphorically, a goat who leaves your ministry or is done with you will mess things up so that nobody else will want to be there. Goats ruin it for others.

God. God is the only unrestricted being in the entire universe. God is the creator of all things. He is without beginning or ending. He is omnipotent, omnipresent, omniscient, and invisible.

Godhead. Godhead is the name given to the unified operation of the Father, the Son, and the Holy Ghost.

God's will. A description of something that matches the desire and design that God has for a person at a particular time and place. It is in keeping with His destiny and purpose. God has made His will known to us in the Bible. There is internal witness, but that is subjective and must come second to the external and objective truth of the Word of God, the Bible. Also, an internal witness must have confirmation, which is agreement by those who are of higher authority and ranking spiritually, that lets a person know that something actually *is* the will of God. If we say that people are in the will of God, we mean they are assured that they are walking the right path and will find themselves in a position ordained by God. It does not always have to be pleasant. However,

G

you can't say that God wants a person to have cancer in order to teach a lesson because the Bible tells us what God's will is, which is in direct opposition to that. "I wish above all things that you would prosper and be in health even as your soul prospers."

Jesus is the physical demonstration of the will of God. The Bible says that God anointed Jesus Christ of Nazareth, and the Holy Ghost empowered Him to do good and heal all who were oppressed of the devil. There is no place in the Bible where Jesus lays hands on somebody and makes the person sick. It stands to reason then that nobody in the Bible needed to be taught anything by being made sick. When you consider this, you realize that it is not the will of God for a person to be sick. It is not, in fact, God's will for people to be poor. It is not God's will for there to be terrible tragedies. The will of God can be made known to us by the Holy Spirit. Spiritual authority and headship should confirm it to us. Not everything that happens is God's will.

Good. Something that is proper, wholesome, true, and favorable.

Good news. The Gospel is good news. When you refer to the Gospel of the kingdom, you are referring to the good news of the kingdom.

Goodness. Goodness is the quality and the state of being that is good in continual motion. It is not a static act of having done something good. It is the quality of being that is continuing good in motion.

G

Gospel. Good news. It relates especially to the books of Matthew, Mark, Luke, and John, which are referred to as the four gospels because they contain the good news.

Gossip. Speaking not *to* someone but *about* someone without the conversation being true, edifying, or necessary.

Governing church. A church that has great authority in a particular region, relating to spiritual warfare, the releasing of ministry gifts, and dealing with the spiritual climate of the region.

Government. Refers to a person's ability to properly manage something. Government carries with it the idea of control and direction of a person, an organization, or a nation in order to determine outcomes.

Grace. The unmerited favor of God. It is linked with words like anointing, *charismas*, and others of that nature. Some things are referred to as grace gifts, which means that God gave you these things by grace. Grace carries with it the implication that something was not earned and probably not deserved; however, because God has favor toward you, He extends benevolence to you based upon His goodness. The five-fold ministry is sometimes referred to as grace gifts. And some of the gifts of the Spirit are referred to as grace gifts as well. In the technical sense, any gift is a gift of grace because it has been given and has not been merited.

Great. To be large or strong in scope.

G

Great commission. A term used to distinguish the words of Jesus. Matthew 28:19 says, "Go ye therefore, and teach all nations, baptizing them in the name of the Father, and of the Son, and of the Holy Ghost." That is referred to as the great commission. The great commission was among the last words that Jesus spoke; he commissioned his disciples and all those who would come later to continue to spread the Gospel of the kingdom and to make disciples of people all over the world.

Greeter. A commonly seen position of ministry in churches. Greeters are those who have a hospitable disposition and who welcome those that come to the church. They shake hands, smile, and welcome people at the door of the sanctuary. (See Ministry of helps.)

Growth. Growth is the positive and forward development that generally occurs incrementally as a result of the operation of the Word, the Spirit, and the purposeful application of life principles by the believer.

Hallelujah. (See Alleluia.)

Hand. When we refer to the hand as a biblical metaphor, it usually refers to the function of the five-fold ministry, which includes the apostle, prophet, pastor, evangelist, and teacher. Sometimes the phrase *hand of God* is used metaphorically to speak of the functions of the ministry as a whole. The Bible says that God will bless what you put your hand to do, such as your work, your functioning, or your labor. Your hand and what you do with it express the intent of your heart. When Abraham came to tithe, he said, "I have lifted up my hand unto the Lord." He recognized that God was the source of his ability to do what he did with his hands.

Happiness. Happiness involves the emotions, and generally something must happen in order to produce it. Joy, however, is different because joy is something that springs from the spirit and requires no external events.

Harlot. A prostitute, a person who has sex for money. It is different from a whore because someone could be a whore without the involvement of money. In the spiritual context, it refers to those who are not exclusive in their covenant with God but interact with a host of philosophies, doctrines, and spirits.

Harvest. Fruition. It is the desired outcome of deeds, seeds, and efforts given into a particular area. It means that you began somewhere with a vision and a dream

H

and a desired outcome, and along the way you did both the big and little things that it takes to produce whatever you desired but did not have when you started. When it comes into reality, it is a harvest.

Hate. An intense dislike or despising of something or someone.

Head. Head is the term or designation given to the ultimate authority of anything.

Head of the household. The head of the household is whoever is responsible for the well-being of that family. It could be a mother, father, grandparent, or adoptive parent, but it is whoever is in the position of authority. He or she is responsible for the decisions made and for the well-being of the others in the family. Because there are many single-parent households, the head need not be a male. Responsibility and authority go hand-in-hand. You cannot be responsible for something over which you do not have authority, and you cannot have authority over something for which you are not responsible.

Headship. The recognition that everything that God creates has distinctions of government, authority, proper position, and functioning. Headship is also a term given to whoever may be directing or leading a family, a group, or an organization that is under proper biblical authority. Just as the faculties for thought, vision, hearing, and speaking are in the human head, headship refers to the one who leads something. Whether it is a home, a business, or a church under proper authority, the head is responsible for and has authority over it in order to direct, hear, speak, and govern it. (See Authority.)

Healing. The returning of the body to a holistic state as a result of prayer and faith.

Hear. To understand.

Heart. The place where the spirit and the soul connect. The interaction between the spirit and the soul is referred to as the heart of man. This is not referring to the physical organ.

Heathen. A person who is without the knowledge of God.

Heaven. The spiritual place from which God rules all. The Bible talks about three different heavens. There is the natural heaven, which is the atmosphere. The second heaven is the spiritual dimension from which the principalities and powers of the air come. Then there is the third heaven, the dwelling place of God, which is sometimes referred to as the City of God. In heaven there is the absence of all evil and the presence of all that is good. Heaven is the eternal dwelling place for all believers.

Hell. Fire does not make hell. That's not to say that there *isn't* fire. What makes hell is the lack of the presence of God. Hell is a place of eternal damnation, which is eternal separation from God. People do not go to hell because God does not love them; people go to hell because they don't love God. People go to hell because they never accepted God's gift, Jesus. Ultimately, this is why people go to hell, not because they lied, cheated, or

H

stole. They lied, cheated, or stole due to their nature; they are dead in their spirit and have separation from God. When they become born again, they get a new nature.

Help. To assist. (See Ministry of helps.)

Helpmeet. Helpmeet is the description given to Eve in her relationship to Adam because she was suitable to help Adam. Sometimes a wife is referred to as a helpmeet; she is suitable for, compatible with, and complimentary to her husband. The Lord God said, "It is not good for man to be alone; I will make a helper suitable for him."

Heresy. A position, doctrine, or opinion that is at odds with what is taught by God's representatives.

Heretic. A person who holds and espouses heresy and who uses it to engage in controversy.

Hermeneutics. The way verses of the Bible relate to other verses of the Bible.

Hinder. To thwart progress and to work against something.

Hindrance. The term given to anything that hinders.

Holiness. The spiritual disposition of maintaining honor and respect toward God and seeking to live life that exemplifies and honors the fact that God has accepted you.

Holy. Holy means separate, and it really means other. When the Bible says that God is holy, it is saying that He is other. No matter what you find, He is other than that. When we say that the tithe is holy, we mean that the ten percent is other than the rest we have. Holy means to be separate and to be distinguished by greater difference. A person, space, or object can be holy in that it can be distinguished and separate because of its greater difference. Holy means sacred.

Holy Ghost, Holy Spirit, Spirit of God. The third person of the Godhead, who appears throughout the Bible in forms and word pictures, such as a dove, water, fire, rain, and oil. The Holy Ghost dwells in believers. The Holy Ghost is the present-day member of the Godhead in action on earth. The Holy Spirit is omnipresent because He is everything that God the Father and Christ are. The Holy Ghost does not necessarily dwell within everybody. When I say that we receive the Holy Ghost, I am referring to the infilling rather than the indwelling. The Holy Ghost can always be called upon for help. The Holy Ghost empowers; in other words, you don't pray to the Holy Spirit, but the Holy Spirit helps you pray. You don't worship the Holy Spirit, but the Holy Spirit helps you worship. (See Baptism of the Holy Spirit.)

Holy of Holies. The place in the Tabernacle of David where the Ark of the Covenant rested. It was separated from the inner court by a veil. Behind that veil, the priest entered once a year on the Day of Atonement. The Holy of Holies is symbolic of the place where you are face-to-face and intimate with God. When you are intimate with God, you are not in the outer court of the physical world or the inner court of the soul relationship, but you are in

H

the Holy of Holies, which means that the veil of the flesh has been torn; you are in a spiritual state of communion with God. The outer court, inner court, and Holy of Holies are, of course, symbolic of body, soul, and spirit. God is communing in the spirit in the Holy of Holies.

Homegoing. A homegoing, a funeral, is the ceremony that takes place at the time of a person's departure from the earth. It is an old-time word.

Homiletic. The way a preacher puts a message together. *Homo-letics* means that the message starts and ends at the same place, and it carries a particular theme. Messages that people in Bible school are taught to preach are homiletic.

Honor. Honor is deference or recognition.

Hope. Different from faith, it is the desire to believe and the subsequent belief in a positive outcome.

House. A term that is frequently used for the church. It implies a group of people under the same roof or covering. It also speaks of family, of belonging to the same house or household.

House of God. A name for church.

Household of Faith. A name given to the church. It is implied when we refer to a church as a family.

Humble. In the positive sense, it means to be in a disposition of thankfulness and gratitude, knowing that what you have accomplished in and through life or what you have in terms of things, influence, or relationships is not a result of your efforts, but rather a result of God's involvement. In the negative sense, to be humbled means to be brought low. You can humble someone, or God can humble someone. We are to be humble, but we can also *be* humbled.

Humility. Humility is the absence of haughtiness, arrogance, and pride. It is the understanding that what you have, who you are, and what you have accomplished are a result of the grace of God on your life.

Hunger. A desire for something.

Husband. A person who gives continual care, oversight, and nurturing to something for which that person has great concern, attachment, and authority. By law, a husband is a man who is married to a wife.

Hymn. A classification of songs that convey doctrine and foundational truth. A hymn is a distinction given to a particular form of song that is about God and that is consistent with doctrinal and theological understandings about God. Singing about "coming to church in the wildwood" is not a hymn. (See Psalm and Spiritual song.)

I wills. Satan's sin of pride is contained in the five *I wills*: I will ascend into heaven, I will exalt my throne above the stars of God, I will sit upon the mount of the congregation, I will ascend above the heights of the clouds, and I will be like the Most High.

Idolatry. The worship of anything other than God. It is also making a god out of something other than God, such as creating an idol by carving something out of rock or wood. There are also idols that are not so overt; some people worship money as their god. Other people have their job as their god or sports as their god. Idols are whatever people worship or put energy toward that causes them to displace and replace God.

Ignorant. Describes people who have *ignor-ance*, which is ignoring something or not having information on something. (See Stupid.)

Image and likeness. The reflection of something else.

Impactive. The effect caused by the operation and activity of a ministry. A ministry with weight, substance, impetus, and momentum is said to have impact. Impact also involves scope. The number of people affected by the operation of a ministry is one indicator of its impact. Impact cannot truly be measured statistically although a ministry with impact will always have results.

I

Impart. To convey to another person what you carry in your spirit.

Impartation. The process of imparting. (See Impart and Transference of spirits.)

Importunity. The persistent, continual action of not giving up.

Impotent. In King James English, it is *im-potent*, meaning the lack of power.

Increase. In part, refers to what God puts in your hand. It is also referred to as first fruits or money. To increase means to grow and to progress. It refers to growth, progression, and prosperity. You can increase in knowledge, wisdom, etc. It can also refer to finances that come into your possession. Tithing is honoring God with the first of your increase.

Indenture. An indentured servant is one who owes the master and is bound by the debt.

Indoctrinate. To indoctrinate is to teach someone principles and precepts in line with a certain school of thought.

Indwelling of the Holy Spirit. (See Baptism of the Holy Spirit.)

Infilling of the Holy Spirit. (See Baptism of the Holy Spirit.)

Inheritance. The benefit you receive by the labor of another. It doesn't necessarily have to do with someone's dying and leaving you an estate. The Bible says that there is an inheritance among the saints. Those who are joined in ministry realize that there is an inheritance that they get by being a part of the ministry. It is gain that is not based on your own labor.

Iniquity. Iniquity is different from the act of sin. Iniquity is the inherent propensity to lean toward sin and evil.

Inner court. The middle place referenced in the tabernacle of David. There was an outer court, an inner court, and the Holy of Holies. The inner court is symbolic of the nature of the soul of man.

Inspiration. The divine spark, motivation, or unction given by God that becomes the basis for action.

Instruction. Instruction differs from teaching or training. Teaching is the communicating of the information. Training is the application of the information, walking it out. Instruction is essentially the how-to. Instruction is the application of principles applied into a particular context. If someone teaches you all night about something in which you have no interest, you receive no actual instruction. You only gain instruction when you apply information to your life. (See Teaching and Train.)

Integrity. Integrity is wholeness. It refers to someone's being the same on the outside and the inside. It is found where there is no break between belief and action. You have integrity if you are not doing one thing on the inside and something else on the outside. Integrity is being

I

what you appear to be and having no hidden agendas. It means that if you say something, you will do it. People trust people who have integrity.

Intercession. To intercede is to come between, to step in to do something, and to exercise a degree of responsibility that is not necessarily incumbent upon you legally. Intercession is taking up someone else's part.

Intercessor. An intercessor is a person who intercedes on behalf of another through prayer.

Intercessory prayer. A prayer made on behalf of someone else. Intercessory prayer does not require the cooperation or even the knowledge of the person being prayed for. A person can be against God and still benefit from intercessory prayer. Sometimes intercession is referred to as standing in the gap. It benefits recipients whether or not they are aware of it. It can be done for somebody who is in dire straits or for somebody who is in great straits. It benefits the giver as well as the receiver.

Intercessory prayer may consist of praying in tongues or praying in the Spirit. It may consist of the groaning or travailing referred to in Romans. Intercessory prayer groups in a church are there to pray in line with the spoken vision of the church, which is the vision that comes to them from headship. The intercession ministry is there to listen to what is being spoken from headship and then to pray that what they've heard will come to pass and come to the point of harvest. Such groups receive prayer assignments that could include people, events, unsaved loved ones, or families that are sick. The intercessors may not personally know the person for whom they are praying. On a larger scale, the intercessors may pray for the children of the city, the well-being of the city itself, people who have addictions, the girls on the street, the betterment of the local house, pastors and their families, finances, and opportunities. Intercessory prayer is prayer made on behalf of another. Once you begin to pray for yourself, you cease to intercede.

Internal witness. The testimony of the Holy Spirit on the inside of a person that bears witness to the truth or accuracy of something.

Interpretive dance. A dance that includes movements set to music, that conveys feelings or impressions, and that is inspired by a song or piece of music.

Into captivity. In the negative sense, this term pertains to people who become captive by getting involved in anything that limits them from doing good. In the positive sense, it is the concept of being willing to be in covenant with someone, to go into captivity with someone. Going into captivity is the voluntary limiting of certain freedoms for a greater purpose. The marriage covenant is an example. When people get married, they are limiting certain freedoms for a greater purpose. The phrase into captivity represents a bond of a positive nature. The Bible tells us, for example, the children of Moab refused to go into captivity. Refusing covenant for convenience, they sacrificed future blessing for momentary convenience. These people were unfit to lead because of their unwillingness to go into captivity with their brothers. Into captivity refers to a strong covenant.

I

Israel. Geographically, Israel is a country on the eastern shore of the Mediterranean Sea. Israel is also a reference to the people of God. It becomes metaphoric of the people who are now the people of God; Christians are sometimes referred to as a spiritual Israel.

Jehovah. Jehovah is a part of the covenant names of God. It implies "the Lord who is" and includes all the suffixes that come after that, such as Jehovah Tsidkenu. *Tsidkenu* means righteousness; the Lord is my righteousness. Jehovah Nissi means the Lord is my banner. Jehovah Rohi means the Lord is my healer. Jehovah Shalom means the Lord is my peace. Jehovah is a prefix for the covenant names of God.

Jerusalem. Israel, Jerusalem, and Zion speak metaphorically and figuratively of the church. Israel means the people of God. Jerusalem means the place of peace. Zion is the place where David set up the temple. Zion speaks of living the higher plane of life; it speaks of the spirit life, which is higher. The Bible refers to the law's going forth out of Zion. The way to Zion is always up; the references to Zion are up. At one point, David appointed singers and dancers. He said, "We are not going to Mount Sinai any longer. Now we are going to Mount Zion." It is not the floating cloud nobody can touch nor God being behind the darkness, as at Sinai. Now we go to Zion; joyfully, gladly, we go up with singing.

Sinai represents the lower life, not negative but lower and incomplete. Zion is the higher life. All of Zion is in Jerusalem, but not all of Jerusalem is in Zion. There are Israel, Jerusalem, and Zion; there is that picture of three again, which parallels the outer court, the inner court, and the Holy of Holies. It also parallels the spirit, soul, and body. Jerusalem is the place of peace. Salem means

J

peace. Zion is the high place; it is where the temple is and where the presence of God is.

Jesus. Jesus is the name given to the earthly vessel in which the Word of God dwelled. The Word of God dwelled in the Son of God. There are other names too: the Bread of Life, the Savior of the world, Emanuel, Christ, the Way, the Truth, the Light, and the Door.

Joy. A fruit of the Spirit. Joy is distinct from happiness. Happiness is a matter of your soul, and something needs to happen to produce it. Joy is something that springs from the spirit within, which needs no external stimuli. It is the state of well-being that surfaces even in the midst of apparent adversity. Joy is of the spirit. Happiness is of the emotions.

Jubilee. The Old Testament law of jubilee required a Sabbath year after every seven years. After the forty-ninth year, the end of seven Sabbaths, the fiftieth year was the year of jubilee. During the year of jubilee, land was returned to its original owner. All the bondservants and indentured servants were set free. Families were reunited. Debts were forgiven. The year of jubilee is a metaphor of what happens when a person receives Christ; the person enters into a proverbial year of jubilee. An ongoing process of restoration, freedom, and deliverance is begun.

Judah. One of the twelve tribes of Israel. Judah is also a name for praise. Jesus was from the tribe of Judah.

Judgment. There is more than one meaning. In the negative sense, it can refer to being under the wrath of God.

In the positive sense, it can mean exercising the ability to make proper decisions. It is the ability to see things for what they are and to make appropriate decisions based on that. Although it is not separate from the spiritual realm, judgment differs from discernment, which is a gift of the Holy Spirit, because judgment involves logic or rational thought processes. Judgment is the putting together of pieces to understand something. Discernment is more like a snapshot in which you see something for what it is. Judgment involves working through it and judging it as you are going along.

Justify. To be declared without fault or blame, to put into a position of never having done wrong.

Kairos. (See Chronos and kairos.)

Keys. They are symbolic and speak of authority and access to principles, understandings, or other things that a person has the ability to lock or unlock for others.

Kingdom churches. Churches that teach a strong message of the rulership of Christ, which should invade all of present culture. Many times the emphasis is on taking dominion now rather than on the afterlife.

Kingdom mysteries. Kingdom mysteries include everything in the kingdom of God that is not apparent to the casual observer; these mysteries take spiritual intuition and insight in order to draw understandings and inferences about how God's rule works in the earth.

Kingdom of chaos. People who are governed by unclean spirits are ingrained into the kingdom of darkness, and their life becomes chaotic. Eventually they find that they live in a kingdom of chaos ruled by the Devil.

Kingdom of darkness. Refers to the domain of authority that Satan inhabits and the hierarchy thereof, which includes principalities, powers, and spiritual wickedness. It is a kingdom with a hierarchy; it is *not* the democracy of darkness.

Kingdom of God. The kingdom of God is the domain of God, and it is the converse of the kingdom of darkness.

K

The kingdom of God is where His Lordship and rule is acknowledged and exercised. The kingdom of Satan is a kingdom of chaos and produces chaos. Concerning the kingdom of God and the kingdom of heaven, there is, by the way, an ongoing theological debate as to whether these are synonymous or not.

Kingdom of light. Any place or spirit influence in which the Word of God and the people of God are in authority.

Knowledge. Knowledge is the highest plane of natural and rational thought. It is above belief. Knowledge is not necessarily a spiritual function. It is not an anti-spiritual function either, but there are things that are only spiritually discerned or known. Knowledge in the natural sense is different from knowledge in the spiritual sense. Knowledge in the natural is touchable or empirical, which means open to view. Knowledge in the spiritual involves discernment and other factors. Knowledge in the natural, rational mind involves some process and the arrival at a point of knowing after having analyzed, gathered, and observed data. Spiritually, knowledge or the discerning of something can be instantaneous because it is not based on empirical or touchable evidence. (See Gift of the word of knowledge.)

Latter days. Refers to a non-specific period of time before the return of Christ when prophetic fulfillment is realized. The culmination of good and evil as signified in wheat and tares comes to harvest season. It is an intense time of simultaneous revival, restoration, and political, economic, and catastrophic problems.

Latter rain. The seasonal rains that come. The early rains prepare the field for the planting of the seed, and the latter rain comes just before the harvest. Metaphorically, the term is used to delineate the latter-day outpourings of the Holy Spirit in modern society, which indicate that we are being prepared for the end-time harvest, the latter-day harvest.

Law. A permanent, fixed principle—a statute. The term is also used in reference to the first five books of Moses, the Pentateuch or the Law. Sometimes it is used in conjunction with the Ten Commandments. It is also used to encompass all of Judaism.

Lawlessness. Unrestrained and unruly; possessing no self-restraint.

Laying on of hands. A method by which one of greater authority blesses, imparts, activates, releases, and administers grace to those of lesser authority.

Leader. A person whose life, actions, or ideas influence the direction of others.

L

Leading of the Holy Spirit. Romans 8 says, "As many as are led by the Spirit of God, they are the sons of God." So the Spirit of God leads us. The leading of the Holy Spirit is the internal witness of the Holy Spirit in the life of believers, causing them to know divine direction and the will of God. This can happen by the reading of Scripture. It can happen through the words of a pastor's preaching. It can happen by understanding providence and circumstance.

Leaven. Leaven in the natural sense is yeast, which causes fermentation in bread dough. Metaphorically, Christians use the word *leaven* to represent sin. When the children of Israel had Passover, they put all of the leaven out of their houses, which was symbolic of the removal of unclean things. When bread is being made, "a little leaven leaveneth the whole lump," which symbolically means that a little bit of something unclean can get into your life, infect it, and have a negative effect upon all of it. Jesus told us to beware of the leaven of the scribes and Pharisees. The Bible refers to the leaven of the scribes and Pharisees as legalism. If you let a little bit of that in, it adversely affects the whole.

Legalism. Legalism is assiduous adherence to the letter of the law of religious principle without regard to the spirit of the law, to the purpose for which the law was written, or for the people to which it was written. It is policy over people.

Liberty. Having liberty is being free. You may feel freedom when you go to a particular church and realize that it is okay if you lift up your hands, if you are dressed up, or if you are just dressed casually. There is liberty there.

You do not feel constrained and bound up. Liberty means being released from negative restraints so that you can move in a positive and purposeful direction in the will of God. Liberty does not mean being without any restraint. It does not mean that you can feel at liberty to scream "fire" throughout a building. The Bible says, "Where the Spirit of the Lord is, there is liberty."

Life. The functioning of the biological body. There is also the word *zoë*, which is translated into English as the word *life* and means the God kind of life or abundant life. It is relationship; it is spiritual. This kind of life begins at conversion, when a person is born again. Life begins and continues to grow as long as you walk in the light and in relationship with God. He who has the Son has life. He who has not the Son has not life. Life also can be defined as the span of time that a person is alive on this planet.

Lifting of hands. A physical action during praise and worship, which denotes surrender, victory, openness, and exaltation to God. Metaphorically, because the hands are symbolic of the heart, hands are considered the tools that fulfill what the heart imagines. So with your hands, you live out what's in your heart. You lift up your hands because you can't get your heart up there.

Also, note that when tithing to Melchizadek, Abraham said, "I have lifted up my hand unto the Lord." That did not necessarily mean that his hand was above his head. It means that his hand was what he worked with, and it was lifted up to the Lord in worship and adoration. In other words, what is in people's hands is there because they recognize that God prospers the work of their hands.

L

Light. Light is the absence of darkness. It is also illumination. It is a by-product of the Word of God. David said that the entrance of God's Word brings light. Light is also the state of walking or living in known illumination. When you are walking in the truth that you know, you are walking in the light. When you walk outside of what you have been taught, you are getting back into the darkness. To walk in ignorance would also be to walk in darkness. If you know the truth and don't walk in it, then you are in darkness.

Lineage. To come from the line of, or of the line of. Lineage is a family tree. It is the history of a family.

Living stones. A term used to describe Christians in reference to their being part of God's building or temple. We are living stones set in order in the house of God.

Living water. Water, as does bread, speaks to the basic necessities of life. A person needs water to live. Spiritually speaking, there is living water, which belongs to the spirit realm and refreshes a person's spirit and soul. Living water is a result of a relationship with God, His Word, and the Holy Spirit; this relationship causes believers to be refreshed and nourished, and it quenches the internal thirst of people.

Living Word. Living Word means the Word of God as it applies to Scripture. The Bible says that the Word of God is alive, quick, and powerful. The Living Word as it applies to Scripture means that the words on the page are more powerful than just words on a page. They are not simply stories and historic accounts, but there is a divine energy behind what is read that makes it *alive* and viable. The Word has creative power within it. It is quick and powerful. It is sharp. It is cutting. It has forward movement to it. It is not just merely existing. (See Rhema.)

Logos. Logos is translated into English as *word.* We get the words *logic* and *logo* from it. Ultimately, it means the mind of the Creator expressed in an image. Jesus can be referred to as the Word or Logos of God. He is the mind, the will, the heart, and the plan of God expressed in an image. This logo represents the mind of the Creator. Jesus is also the logic of God, which means that if you want to know what God thinks about something, you only have to look at Jesus. What does God think about healing? Well, what did Jesus do? He went about doing good and healing all those oppressed of the Devil. This supports the argument that you cannot logically say that God wants you to be sick, because God gave you His logic, which includes the healing of Jesus. So Jesus is the Logos, the logic of God. Jesus is the rationale of God in flesh. He is the expressed image, the logo of the heart, the mind, and the plan of God.

Longsuffering. Longsuffering is a fruit of the Spirit. Longsuffering means to suffer for a long time. It is the quality of being able to endure circumstances and to tolerate the idiosyncrasies and problematic areas of people while you yet believe in the good in them. It is *not* being dysfunctional and letting people be stupid. You had better have the quality of longsuffering if you want to be a pastor. But this word doesn't have a victim quality. Being longsuffering does not mean saying, "This is my cross to bear." It is a positive movement. It is a fruit of the Spirit that you develop over time, a quality that

L

comes from the Spirit and that sees ultimate good; therefore, you are able to put up with circumstances and people's idiosyncrasies. You can move forward without their causing you great angst all of the time. It doesn't mean long torture. *Suffer* is old English for *allow*. Think of the following verses, for example: "Suffer the little children to come unto me" and "The kingdom of heaven suffereth violence," which means that the kingdom of heaven allows violence. There is an allowance given here. Longsuffering is allowing a circumstance to be as it is without its killing you. You are longsuffering when you are allowing others to be. This word could also be referred to as *longallowance*. (See Fruit of the Spirit.)

Looking for my brothers. Comes from the story of Joseph, who was sent by his father to find his brothers. It is the concept that we should keep our eyes open for people who may be connected to us though we do not know it yet. Also, we really shouldn't be connected to some of the people that we think that we should be, and we are already connected to some people that we have yet to find out about. The term implies realizing that some people may not look like they are connected to you; they may appear hard, distant, or unsavory, but you have to be big enough to realize that they may be your brothers and that neither of you know yet.

Loose. To be loose is to be free from bondage, constraints, and imprisonment in your mind, heart, or soul. (See Bind.)

Lord's prayer. The origin is in Matthew 6, where Jesus taught the disciples how to pray.

L

Lord's table. Refers to communion. It is the celebration of communion through the taking of bread, commemorating the Lord's body, and the taking of the cup, representing the Lord's blood.

Love. Three separate words are translated into the single English word *love*. First, p*hileo* is the love one brother has for another. It is the origin of the name Philadelphia, which is the city of brotherly love. Second, *eros* is the origin of the word *erotic*. It is sensual, sexual love. Third, *agape* refers to the kind of love, unconditional and spiritual, that God has for you.

Lying spirit. An evil entity that causes a person to tell things that are not truthful. Sometimes it can cause people to lie even when telling the truth would benefit them more. When people have a full manifestation of a lying spirit, they may not even know when they are telling a lie. They are deceived and may actually believe that their lies are truth.

Magnify. To enlarge in your sight, to make bigger.

Manifestation. The tangible reality of something.

Manna. Bread. It is a reference to the children of Israel, who received manna from God every morning when they got up. When the manna came, they could only get it once a day, and the people had to get their own. Manna would only last for one day. If they kept it until the next day and tried to eat it, it would have worms in it. Metaphorically speaking, it means that every day you should have something fresh from God in your heart and in your mind. There are people who try to live on what is called yesterday's manna. They are trying to reheat something that was good and accurate for yesterday, instead of making it alive today. The Word of God should be fresh and alive to you every day. You should not live off previous knowledge or religious routine that is not really alive to you.

Mantle. A garment. It is metaphoric and symbolic of the anointing and position carried by the person who wears it. It is something that people wear, not something they do. It is something they carry with them at all times. A person can receive someone else's mantle; think of Elijah and Elisha. After being under someone's authority, a person can carry the same kind of spirit. Having some-one else's mantle in its fullest context does not occur until after the senior person has died; then the person who received the mantel can begin to stand in place of

M

the senior person and develop characteristics that came from the mentoring.

Marriage. Biblically defined as a man and a woman entering into a legal and spiritual covenant.

Marvelous. A quality that causes people to be amazed.

Maturity. Something matures when it comes to completion or to a state of fulfillment; then it has maturity.

Measure. Involves amount. People have a measure of faith. People have a measure of authority. It involves the amount or scope given to someone or had by someone.

Measure of authority. Measure of authority is defined by the speed and scope at which one can initiate or prohibit. Jesus referred to this as binding and loosing. Your authority, therefore, is recognizable to others by 1) what you can set into motion or what you can stop and 2) the size, scope, or number of people it affects. (See Forward untangling and Bind.)

Mediate. To put yourself between two opposing parties and seek to bring peace.

Meditate. To think on something and to turn it over and over in your mind and heart. The act of meditation.

Meekness. A fruit of the Spirit. It is strength under control. Meekness is the ability to properly direct and restrain your power and authority for good. Meekness is not weakness. You need strength to apply meekness. To be meek is to have things under control.

Mentor. A person who has skill in an area or life experience and helps someone who is in the process of learning it.

Mercy. Benevolence and favor where it is not earned. This does not mean, however, that it is not merited by the situation.

Mighty Counselor. One of the names of distinction given to Christ.

Mind. The seat and government of the soul. The soul includes the emotions, the mind, the will, and the intellect. The mind is not the brain. The mind is the place of self-consciousness and the seat of self, personality, and thought.

Minister. To serve. It is also a title that is given to those in the church who serve in a particular field for the betterment of the flock.

Ministry. The name given to the ongoing function of outreach and to people's functioning in their grace gift and in their calling toward another.

Ministry of helps. Includes whatever is done to help the ministry. It is lending ability, time, resources, energy, finances, or talent to forward the cause and the purpose of God by eliminating the need for those of higher authority to do what others are capable of doing. Ushers are in the ministry of helps; people duplicating the tapes are in the ministry of helps. The people who teach the children's ministry, the greeters, the singers, and the praise team are all in the ministry of helps. They are using their time, energy, and resources to forward the cause by doing something so that those of higher authority may give attention to other things. (See Forward untangling and Armorbearer.)

Ministry of maintenance. A role that people, especially pastors, can fall into. They allow their energy to be consumed by maintaining people at their current level rather than leading them to the next level or to where they should be going. Moses had a ministry of maintenance. Every morning the people received the manna miracle. They had shoes that didn't wear out. They had water from a rock. And Moses maintained them while they walked in the wilderness for forty years. There are people who do not grow and who constantly seek to be maintained in life, spiritually, materially, or both. Although there shouldn't be, there are people who seek to minister to those who refuse to go to the next level; these ministers waste their resources that could have been better invested in people who are willing to grow and prosper in the body of Christ. (See Get off my boat.)

Ministry of reconciliation. The priestly ministry in which we reconcile people with God and people with each other.

Minstrel. A person who plays a musical instrument and who is able to create a proper atmosphere, which invokes the presence of God as they play.

Miracle in motion. The concept that the fulfillment of a miracle may have been initiated in the spirit realm, even though you can't see it yet. Miracle in motion is an awareness that the miracle has begun and that the miracle *is in motion*. Something is working. It's coming. Don't give up. (See Step of faith.)

Miracles. Unexplainable, awe-inspiring, supernatural events that override natural laws and predicted outcomes.

Mission. A place where people can rest, find sanctuary, and have physical needs (food, shelter, clothing, and warmth) met; people receive this with hopes of being restored to a productive life. A mission also can be defined as a corporate objective. It is an envisioned outcome that fits into a grander scheme of things.

Missionary dating. A term that means a Christian is dating a non-Christian and using the excuse that the non-Christian will begin to believe in Jesus due to the Christian's influence. It is a rationalization to justify pursuing a situation that should not be pursued.

Missions. Taking the Gospel to foreign fields, or any area or people with which the missionary does not normally associate. Missions outreaches do not always have to be to a foreign field; they simply need to be to people or places that have a need for the Gospel. Missions involves the strengthening of other people. Missions is different from evangelism, though there is a connection between the two. Missions many times involves temporarily meeting material needs. Many missions outreaches involve doctors and the giving of food.

Momentum. Involves the unseen yet discernible forward movement and impetus of something that has acceleration and power moving it toward its desired goal.

M

Agreement, unity, and the number of victories or right things occurring in succession build spiritual momentum.

Money. Currency. It is also the representation of your life and energy.

More than a conqueror. A conqueror is a person who wins. More than a conqueror refers to a person who leaves a battle with more than he or she brought into battle. People could win a battle yet leave with what they came with or even leave with less than they came with, but people who are more than conquerors leave with more than they came with. The term speaks of going through a circumstance in life and coming out on the other side with more than you went into it with. Understanding, peace, friends, or something else could be added to your life as a result of the battle or circumstance; then you are more than a conqueror. We as Christians are more than conquerors through Him who loves us.

Mountain. Symbolic in the Bible of places of authority and obstacles.

Mountain moving. Mountain moving is the process by which people overcome obstacles and do things that other people have thought impossible. It is achieving goals. It is plowing through. It is creative. It is restorative. It is the process of developing and doing things that other people did not think could be done.

Mourn. To lament over something as if it is dead.

M

Move of God. A widespread flow or emphasis in which God highlights a particular direction, theological understanding, or operation of His Spirit.

Mystery. Something that is hidden from casual observance or that requires revelation to see. Mystery can also be defined as something that requires other pieces of information in order for the proper conclusion to be obvious; an example is the mysteries of the kingdom. You have to know A, B, and C to come up with the full understanding. Even when all the pieces of the mystery are available, it can still be a puzzle until you finally realize how the pieces connect.

Natural. Material and physical. Pertaining to the material, earthly world.

Need. That which is created by lack. You have real needs, and you have perceived needs. Need is the position of not enough. Need and the desire to fill the need cause a person to operate from a position of weakness. The person doesn't move forward. Part of the motivation for moving forward is to fulfill a real or a perceived need, but people who are concentrating on their lack lose better judgment as to what they are doing.

Negativity. A spiritual disposition that causes people to be pessimistic, to see the worst-case scenario, and in general to be robbed of their faith.

Networks. Loose-knit fellowships, groups of churches, or ministries that share their collective resources, knowledge, and understanding.

Neutral. A spiritual disposition of being neither for nor against, but stationary.

New season. The awareness in a person, church, group of people, or family that the close of a particular phase, level, or season of life has come, and now a new season has begun. A new season is earmarked by the refreshing feeling of elation and a spiritual understanding that a particular level has been completed and that something fresh and new has come. (See Next level.)

N

New wine. Used metaphorically to refer to new flows, operations, manifestations, and seasons of the Holy Spirit. The new wine is unpredictable. Its taste, strength, and effect are not known. When the disciples exited the Upper Room on the Day of Pentecost, the townspeople thought the disciples were drunk with new wine, something they were not used to and of which they could not accurately judge the strength. The embracing of new flows of the Spirit can sometimes cause individuals or entire churches to struggle for proper equilibrium. New wine must have new wineskins—a new form or structure that is pliable and flexible to handle the life-giving flow of the Spirit.

Next level. The place that a person is pointed toward, the place directly in front. It may not be the person's ultimate goal or destiny, but it is the next step forward. Technically, your next level is wherever you are going to be next. It is positive because it is the next step, place of understanding, or spiritual awakening on the way to your ultimate destiny. (See New season.)

Now moment. Faith lives in the now. For faith to be operative it has to have a *now* moment. It has to have a moment when all of your believing comes to a point. It is the instant that faith is produced, becomes substance, and is released.

Numbers. The study of the importance of things that are numbered and of their greater significance as it relates within a given situation or Bible story.

Obedience. Walking in the truth that you know. Some people think to obey a command means that you did not want to obey at first. This is a common misconception, which refers to submission, not obedience. Obedience simply means to have an affirming and agreeing spirit and a corresponding action to the will of God. Obedience that demands an explanation is the beginning of rebellion.

Observation. Could be called the principle of observation. It is the ability to draw inference and instruction from something that is seen.

Offend. To sin. Also means to be injurious to another.

Offense. The violation of what you know to be the right thing to do. Also the act of offending people. An offense is the occasion on which you are offended.

Offering. A monetary gift given to a person or organization based upon the discretion of the giver. (See Reciprocity.)

Old wineskins. The term is a metaphor for old, inflexible ways of doing things. This includes thought processes, systems of operation, things that have become outdated, and things that have become staid and immovable. (See New wine.)

O

Open heavens. The concept of living under the blessing of God and of being in right standing with Him. As it relates to spiritual climates, it is being in a position where the atmosphere is conducive to God's purposes and to divine actions taking place. Being under open heavens is the concept that God opens the windows of heaven and pours out a blessing. When you are under open heavens, what is in heaven falls freely to you on earth. It is an atmosphere of being unhindered.

Operation. It means for something to be functional and in motion, as opposed to being static or in theory.

Opportunity. A door of access that is given at a particular time. Opportunity is what God gives and the devil steals.

Outpouring. A particular manifestation of the Holy Spirit's activity. We can say that there is an outpouring of miracles or an outpouring of healing. Outpouring implies an overflow. It implies abundance. It implies a surplus of spiritual activity.

Outreach. Activity outside of church to reach the unchurched.

Overcome. To come over. To overcome something is to run it down. It can mean to run something down, to catch up with it, and overtake it as in a race. Something can also be overcome, overpowered, and defeated in a struggle.

Overtake. To run down and tackle. The Bible says that the blessings of God will overtake you. They will run you down and tackle you. You can't outrun them. Also, you can overtake your enemy. You can run him down and tackle him.

Ownership. God is in a position of ownership of the earth. He put man in a position of stewardship of the earth. Ownership also means to possess something as one's own. To have ownership is to rightfully possess something, such as information, ideas, concepts, or understandings. People can regurgitate another person's information and not be in ownership of it if they just put it out without any thought or understanding of it.

Parent. Someone from whom offspring have come; the parent is responsible for the offspring.

Passive. Passive is akin to being neutral. To be passive implies that either one does not want a struggle of some kind or does not want to take the responsibility of knowing something. Being passive is abdicating. Passive people couldn't care less. (See Ahab spirit.)

Passover. One of the feasts of Israel. It refers to the protection from the last plague. The blood of the lamb was applied to the door of the house, and God said He would *pass over* that door and not allow the destroyer to enter.

Pastor. (See Five-fold ministry.)

Peace. Peace is not the absence of conflicts or storms. Peace is the internal quality of remaining unalarmed, unafraid, and secure even in the midst of great adversity or storms. It is the absence of strife internally. To be at peace with something is to not have any hostility toward it. For example, you can be at peace with the will of God. You can be at peace with your environment. You can be at peace with a person.

Pentecost. A feast of Israel that means fiftieth. It is fifty days after Passover. In the book of Acts, the day of Pentecost was when the Holy Spirit was poured out after the resurrection of Christ and where the believers began to speak with other tongues.

P – R

Perish. Being robbed of potential. To decrease and then ultimately to become non-existent. The Bible says that where there is no vision the people perish.

Persecute. To be in opposition to and to attack someone due to a difference in views.

Perverse spirit. An evil spirit that causes something's intended use to be turned into another use.

Perversion. Perversion is the twisting, turning, or mis-appropriation of something from its designed purpose or intent.

Pharisee. One who is self-righteous and filled with reli-giosity, whether that person was alive in biblical times or is alive in the present day. Pharisees are also legalistic.

Phileo. Love, as in brotherly love. The word Philadelphia, which means city of brotherly love, comes from *phileo.* (See Love.)

Pious judgment. To judge another person harshly in order to make yourself appear more holy.

Platform. A platform can refer to the stage area in a church. Metaphorically, a platform is also the content of what is spoken. It also refers to the height and breadth to which people are able to speak. Some people's plat-form is greater than that of others. Your performance determines your platform.

Point of contact. Using something material to release a person's faith into the *now* moment, which means at this place and time. The Bible said that prayer cloths, which were actual pieces of cloth, were taken from the body of the apostle Paul and given to people, and they were healed. Sometimes a preacher can't get to everyone, so he might make little swatches of cloth, pray over them, and then give them to people. There is nothing special about the cloths, but these prayer cloths become a point of contact in a *now* moment. A person's faith must be released, and that can happen at the moment the cloth is received. Saying "One day I'm going to believe" or "I used to believe" does not work. All faith has to come into a *now* moment for it to work. In the Bible, a woman said that if she could touch the hem of Jesus' garment she would be made whole. When she touched the hem of His garment, it became a point of contact. It released her faith.

Poor. To be without, to be in lack, and to be disenfranchised. It has a spirit attached to it. Being broke is a temporary economic condition, but poverty is a spirit. Having a spirit of poverty is internal, and it has external manifestations. Poor doesn't just refer to money; it can involve other things as well.

Poor in spirit. This is not the same as the spirit of poverty. During the Sermon on the Mount, Jesus said, "Blessed are the poor in spirit." Poor in spirit means you are able to recognize your own need. Blessed is the person who is able to recognize his or her own need. Some people may not recognize that they are poor in spirit, and, therefore, they may not become blessed because they have no concept of their own need. People cannot receive what they think they already have. You cannot be healed until you admit that you are sick. You cannot be saved until you know that you are not saved. This can be referred to as the positive power of a negative confession. You can't get better until you know that there is something wrong. The poor in spirit are blessed because they are able to recognize their own need and, therefore, be in a position to have it fulfilled.

Positions of strength and weakness. This concept involves the idea that people deal with each other either out of strength or out of weakness. There is a way to determine whether a relationship is built on strength or on weakness. You should always seek to live and to respond from a position of strength rather than from weakness. Weakness is the negative side of your nature. Attaching to someone due to need, lashing out due to anger, or doing something for revenge are all positions of weakness. When we feel we are lacking something, we are acting out of a position of weakness. Acting from strength is the higher road. It is doing something for a positive reason. Function out of an area of strength in your life; do something because you have an abundance, not because you have need for self-fulfillment.

Possessed. A person who is under domination by demonic influence. This person has lost possession of his or her own vessel.

Poverty. Poverty is a spirit that produces a lack of material possessions, as well as feelings of victimization, anger, addiction, facilitation of crime, and the fragmenting of relationships.

Power. Ability to act. To be in the position of causing things to happen rather than being affected by random happenings. To have option and opportunity. To be able. To be authorized. The absence of weakness.

Praise. The conscious choice to be thankful, be jubilant, and celebrate the good works of God. Thinking on past victories can provoke praise. It can also be prophetic. Christians can rejoice over what will happen because they are so convinced of a good outcome that they do not wait until it is fully manifested to praise. (See Prophetic praise.)

Praise team. The members of a church who lead the congregation into praise and worship. This group of people can be distinct from the choir and band. Some churches refer to the praise team as those who sing on microphones, but it can be all-encompassing, including the band, choir, those who sing on microphones, and so forth. Usually though, we refer to the band as the band, the choir as the choir, and the praise team as those with microphones.

Pray. To beseech, to ask. To pray is to enter into communication with God. Prayer also involves communion, thanksgiving, and fellowship; it does not *always* have to be asking for something. To pray means to enter into communion, conversation, and fellowship with God; needs or requests are made known, praise or thanksgiving is offered, emotions and concerns are expressed, and the voice of the Holy Spirit is heard. Prayer is the words that are spoken that articulate those thoughts, intents, concerns, and desires.

Prayer closet. A place to shut yourself away so that you are not drawing attention to yourself when you pray;

then other people are not aware of what you are doing.
The term is used to describe the concept of having a
place of prayer that is private and not for public view.
Then other people cannot hear you. A prayer closet is
secret. It can be any space that is private. Although some
people do so, you don't have to make it a holy room that
you set apart in your house. Some people just have a
particular place where they pray in their house. That is
their prayer closet, which means that all they do there is
pray.

Prayer language. (See Tongues.)

Prayer of agreement. Aligns you with the belief and
desires of another person as you pray for their fulfillment.

Prayer of faith. A prayer of faith is not expressing your
feelings to God. Sometimes you may pray in despair or in
fear, or you may just be relating to God your concerns
and feelings. But the prayer of faith is when you set
yourself in agreement with the will and the purpose of
God, and you pray the answer, not the problem; you
have determined that what you prayed for will come to
pass regardless of contradictory evidence. The prayer of
faith is *not* saying, "Oh God, my daughter's on drugs,
and I don't know what to do about it. I'm asking you to
help her. Please help her." That is a negative and hurtful
thing to do. In relationship with God, it is not wrong to
express to God that emotion, that hurt, that feeling, but
it will not make anything good happen. The prayer of
faith gets through all of that and says, "God never said
my child was an alcoholic. God never said my daughter
was a drug addict. This is *not* what God has said. I

believe that this child is a gift from God, and His promise over her life is that she will be blessed and successful. I stand on God's Word and agree with that, and I resist that which would speak to the contrary. I thank God." A prayer of faith is an affirmative statement to God rather than a complaint about a circumstance.

Praying in the Holy Ghost. Praying in the Spirit, praying in your prayer language.

Preach. To preach is to proclaim. It is the act of proclaiming a message. It is different from teaching because preaching must carry a motivational quality, certain intensity and dynamic that move the listeners beyond the cerebral into an immediate sensing, discerning, and understanding of the things being spoken. Teaching may be motivational, but when something is preached to you, you *get* it more than you intellectually process it. Preaching moves you because it has a certain intensity and push to it.

Precept. A principle of life, a life standard and lesson by which a person can live and build upon. It is something that is always so. It is real. Something that is merely a good saying is not a precept.

Preparation. Readiness for opportunity.

Presbytery. Refers to those in authority. It is the established and recognized headship ministry. Presbytery means being governed by that ministry rather than by congregational rule. This is not limited to the Presbyterian sect; however, it does have to do with that form of government. There is also a real, practical kind of extra-biblical, modern understanding whereby churches have a spiritual operation sometimes called presbytery. The pastor may say, "We want everyone to come to service on Monday night because we are going to have a presbytery." It is supposed to be sober, not somber but sober. People are supposed to take it seriously. Some people will fast and pray for it. Presbytery means that those who are designated as having authority will participate in praying for people, giving instruction, and speaking one on one; what you receive in presbytery is supposed to be received as from the Lord. If a church is going to have a presbytery with just the pastors, people come with that in mind and worship for a while. A pastor may step forward and say that he has a word for this person or that person. It may be about something that the pastor knows from personal knowledge and counsel, or it may be a result of the gifts of the Spirit—a word of knowledge. But either way, your being there means that you are ready to receive what is said to you as coming from the Lord. You don't necessarily know for whom God may give the pastor a word. He is there, and it just comes to him. People are supposed to come with the attitude that what they hear is from the Lord. This whole process is called presbytery, and it can be very powerful.

Presence of the Lord. The presence of the Holy Spirit. It is a term used in Christianity to convey the understanding that the Holy Spirit is dwelling tangibly with people. It is something that is said to convey that God is with us; He is tangible and discernible.

Press in. To press in is to go beyond your comfort zone and to push beyond fatigue or barriers in order to arrive at a spiritual place. Sometimes people in a service are a little tired, or their minds are wandering. The pastor knows that they need to get to a certain level before he can start teaching them, so he may tell them, "Press in a little bit." This means focus, pay attention, and push on beyond what is comfortable in the natural man into what we are doing.

Prevail. To impose yourself to the point of gaining your will. To overcome in a struggle, conflict. To engage in conflict or opposition and yet achieve a desired outcome.

Pride. Focus on self. You are full of pride when you are so focused on yourself that you think everybody's thinking about you. Pride is a high or inordinate opinion of your own dignity, comportment, or superiority. Pride is an inordinate self-focus.

Priest. The Bible mentions both king and priest. The king ministered or spoke to the people on behalf of God, and the priest spoke to God on behalf of the people. The priest served the people by receiving their sacrifices, offerings, prayers, and confessions and by taking those things to God. Jesus is referred to as our High Priest. We are referred to as kings and priests unto our God. So the real priestly ministry is to minister to God on behalf of people and to seek to connect God and people in a practical, experiential way. Priests bear others' burdens.

One of the foundation stones of the Reformation of 1517 was the priesthood of all believers, a theological concept. Before then, people believed, due to Catholicism, that only the priest has access to God. People believed that they had to go through a priest to get to God. When the reformation began, believers realized that they have access to God through Jesus. So we are all kings and priests. To be a priest is to assume and to accept the responsibility for the well-being and benefit of another person, and through your own selflessness, sacrifice, and ministry to them and for them, you seek to bring that person into a better state of being. One of the distinctions of us Christians in the New Testament is that we are a kingdom of priests. So we are all supposed to be taking people that we assume responsibility for and saying, "I'm going to do something sacrificially," not as asceticism but as a sacrifice to them, for them, and around them. Decide that you will do whatever is needed to help bring them into a better state of being. Say, "I'm going to be their priest until I connect them with God."

Principles of the kingdom. Every kingdom has laws and principles that govern activity in that sphere of influence. In the kingdom of God, there are set principles and statutes and fixed ways of functioning that believers should understand. Sowing and reaping is an example: "Be not deceived, God is not mocked. Whatsoever a man soweth that shall he also reap." That is a principle of the kingdom. Principles are designed for things to get better and better. Principles work with both positive and negative factors. If you sow weeds, you are going to reap weeds. If you sow discord with people, you will have a life of discord. Principles should be used for their better purpose; you should learn not to sow weeds or discord, but rather to sow positive things. Principles work arbitrarily. Consider the law of gravity. It works without regard for anyone's belief or station in life. Whether you are red, yellow, black, or white, if you jump off of a building, you are going to hit the ground. So it is with sowing and reaping. The principle that says give and it shall be given unto you, and a hundred other principles that are in the kingdom, function without your involvement. They function without regard for faith, understanding, or spiritual condition. They are laws. It is just so.

Principles that change at the cross. Some things come to the cross and change from a natural understanding to a spiritual understanding. The concept of circumcision is an example. (See Cross.)

Principles that die at the cross. The cross is referred to as a hermeneutic filter, which involves this concept: The cross is the crossroads or the pivotal point of human existence as it relates to Christianity. Everything relates to the arrival and the position of the cross. Some things come to the cross and are completed. Old Testament dietary laws are an example. They come to the cross and die because they are fulfilled. They served their purpose for whatever time, and now they are finished. (See Cross.)

Principles that pass through the cross unchanged. There are things that come to the cross and pass through unchanged. The principle of praise and worship is an example. If you look at the methodology and understanding that we have of praise and worship, it very much mirrors what David did in Psalms: clapping, lifting hands, shouting, dancing, and singing. There was really no need for that to change, so it passed through the cross unchanged. (See Cross.)

Promise. To promise is to state what you will do at a future time.

Promotion. Moving into a higher level of authority and responsibility. It is the result of faithfulness in the last level, growth, and recognition by people of headship authority who release you into a particular area of ministry. It is also gained by battles won. You qualify for promotion through enduring difficult circumstances and through passing tests.

Prophecy. Foretelling, forth telling. A declaration of a *now* word from God. Prophecy is a word that is spoken under the inspiration of the Spirit; it is not a construction of the person speaking it. Prophecy, at its basic level, is exhortation, edification, and comfort. In its highest form, it is creative. It is a gift of the Holy Spirit.

Prophetic insight. The spiritual ability to see the purpose of God in any given context. Though some have a degree of this manifestation that can be exercised as demand is placed upon it, most of the time it operates as the Holy Spirit wills it and allows our eyes to be opened to it.

Prophetic praise. Praise that has the ability to create. It is not praising because something has happened. It is praise that *initiates* something to happen. It occurs when (having believed and prayed for a desired outcome) you begin to praise God for an outcome before it happens; you praise as if it has already happened, and the praise, therefore, becomes creative and causes the outcome to happen.

Prophet's reward. Plenty in the midst of famine.

Prosperity. Ongoing increase. You can have areas of lack and still be prospering because prospering involves movement. It is incremental. You can say, "My goal is there. I am prospering toward that goal. I have increase that is in motion." Too many of us focus on the shortfalls and negatives in life. There are too many folks who spend a lot of time concentrating on lack and keep thinking that they do not and will not have prosperity. Recognize the areas in which you do well, and identify the gains you actually are making. Then put your attention on doing those things that will increase those gains. Remember that prosperity is continuing increase. It is not the total absence of lack. (See Miracle in motion.)

Prostrate. To lie horizontally. To lie as though dead.

Prove me offering. Malachi 3 is the only place in the Bible where we are told to test and prove God, and it involves the area of tithing and offerings. " 'Prove me now herewith,' says the Lord of hosts. 'See if I will not open up for you the windows of heaven, and pour you out a blessing that there is not room enough to receive.' " A *prove me* offering takes place when a person gives an offering with the intent of proving that God is able to meet his or her needs. It is a step of faith, a point of contact. It is an action.

Proverb. It is like a precept, but it has a little something else to it. A precept is just laid out there, but a proverb has either a story or a rhyme to it. A proverb involves didactic sayings. It implies teaching. It is a concise saying that represents truths and life lessons.

Provision. What one has to fulfill the vision. Food and money are examples. Anything that you need to fulfill the vision is provision.

Psalm. Psalms and proverbs are didactic sayings with a teaching quality to them. Proverbs are especially, but psalms are not just praise; they are also instruction put to music. The music is supposed to help you praise God and remember the principles of God. (See Hymn and Spiritual song.)

Psalmist. A person who sings and/or writes music.

Pull/demand. (See Demand on the anointing.)

Pulpit. Refers to the speaking of the church. It doesn't necessarily mean the speaking of God or the speaking of the Pope. Something from the pulpit is something from that level of authority. The pulpit refers to the official stand, leverage, and weight of the church behind a message. Also, some people refer to the entire platform or stage from which people speak as the pulpit. Practically, it is a piece of church furniture or the podium behind which the minister or speaker stands.

Purpose. The reason for something.

Pursue. To go after something with intent.

Rank. Rank refers to position, especially as it relates to authority and placement within the body of Christ.

Rapture. Belongs to the study of eschatology, which refers to the end times. Rapture is the belief that at the

Second Coming of Christ believers will be bodily taken out of the earth. This is not a doctrine, however, because the word *rapture* is not in the Bible. The doctrine is the Second Coming of Christ; Jesus said, "I will come again." Rapture is a subsequent theory. A good end-times doctrine and theology is this: God wins and the Devil loses. (See Kingdom churches.)

Rebellion. To purposely go against something, especially against established authority or truth.

Rebuke. To speak sharply in an effort to bring correction or to stop the continuation of the direction, intent, thoughts, or actions of a person.

Receive. A state of mind that is open to and accepting of what is being conveyed. You can receive a ministry gift or a word spoken. You can choose whether or not to receive a message. You can choose whether or not to receive people by either accepting or rejecting them, by either being open to them or not open to them. Another definition of receive refers to the verse that tells us that as we give we will also receive. The Bible says, "Be not deceived, God will not be made a fool out of. Whatsoever a man soweth, that shall he also reap. He will receive back that which he sows."

Receptive. The quality or the state of having openness and acceptance to what is being communicated.

Reciprocity. The law of reciprocity is the scriptural equivalent of the law that states every action has an equal and opposite reaction. It is the spiritual law of sowing and reaping. Reciprocity has to do with exchange.

Something is given, and something is received. It is not just a one-way thing; it is reciprocal. What you put out, you do get back. It could be positive or negative. Sowing and reaping is just that: If you sow it, you grow it. It is a permanent and fixed law built into the spiritual realm. What you put out, good or bad, is what you will receive back.

Recompense. To pay someone back for something.

Reconciliation. Implies that there was first a separation between two parties. Another party removed the hostility, the barrier, or the offense and brought the parties into a position of one, a position of agreement. This is what Jesus did between man and God. The ministry of reconciliation is the priestly ministry in which we reconcile man with God and man with each other.

Redeemed. To be bought back.

Reformation. Involves the historical time frame that began with Martin Luther in 1517. Reformation means to "re-form." It is the process of taking spiritual principles, the Word of God, and the context of the time frame in which one lives and causing staid concepts and fossilized thinking to be remolded into something that is pliable and applicable, relevant and current for the day in which one lives. The priesthood of all believers is one of the major tenets of the Reformation of 1517. This reformation also involved justification by faith rather than works, the end of indulgences, and the end of the supremacy of the church. This reformation was essentially a reaction to Catholicism. One of the things that Luther taught was the ordination and validation of all vocations. Before that time, it was believed that only priests had a vocation that was pleasing to God. Up to that time, work was almost symbolic of being under a curse. Everyone else had to work, but the priests had a special place. God favored them. But as a result of this reformation, all work was considered sacred. Whatever work you do, do it as unto the Lord. God has blessed you to do it.

Regeneration. Regeneration is part of the work of salvation, which takes place when a person is born again. This person is said to be regenerated. The root word is *gene,* to be *re-gene-erated,* which implies that the spiritual genetics are re-made so that people by nature carry the attributes of the Father. By nature, Christians know to do right; they don't need to try to do right through a position of works. People become good when they are regenerated.

Reign. The scope of God's sphere of dominance.

Rejoice. To stir your spirit and soul though music, praise, testimony, or reflection and then to move your physical body to express the resulting joy.

Relationship. The bearing, measurability, and proportion that one thing has on another. In physical terms, relationship refers to the nature of interaction between parties. It is the correlation that one thing has to another.

Release. Having the authorization by authority to do something. Release also means an outgo from someone. A pastor in a service could say that he is going to release a particular anointing. A person can also be released to do something, but in this sense, releasing someone to do something doesn't necessarily involve a contract. It involves the concepts of headship, authority, and decently and in order; people have to be released and blessed by their superior to perform a certain act or action.

Release of the anointing. The moment, occasion, time, and way in which people become aware that the internal unction, anointing, empowerment, and benefit that they have is now spiritually moving from them to others. It is a positive transference of the Spirit. It can be done in many ways. A person can be preaching and all of a sudden feel that the anointing is being released; people are getting it. Sometimes it is released by the laying on of hands, or someone could be singing and really release the anointing. (See Anointing and Anointing, law of.)

Religion. An organized system of rituals and codes and observances. Religion says that these things need to be observed in order to please God.

Religiosity. Involves things that masquerade as something spiritual but that are in reality legalistic, fixed ideas that stand between man and God. Religiosity relies heavily on form and structure without supplying anything of substance or merit. The word *religious* means rote and implies a lack of thinking or understanding. Religious does *not* mean spiritual and, in fact, usually means just the opposite. Spirituality is man following God. Religiosity is man following man.

Renew. To make new again.

Repent. To repent is not just to feel sorry. It actually means to turn and go in another direction. It is the understanding that your present direction is wrong and unprofitable, so you go in another direction.

Report. A report is a communication that you receive about something you have not seen and do not have personal understanding of. It implies reliance upon the communicator. Whether it is good or evil, it is based on what it produces in the ears of the hearer and in the heart of the giver.

Reputation. What people say about you. (See Character.)

Resident anointing. For every public gathering or worship service of believers, the Holy Spirit has a will for what should be accomplished. The preparing of the hearts of the people and the atmosphere is essential to success. The discerning of the mood and atmosphere created by the will of the Holy Spirit is the resident anointing. Those who are leading the service need to be sensitive to the pace and the ethos of the Spirit. If people work against the resident anointing, they may feel they are swimming upstream—against the current. Trying to motivate people to praise when the resident anointing is for worship can be tiring. The resident anointing is the anointing that is present for a particular purpose. In some instances, if the people are trained and activated in a particular dimension, a resident anointing may rest in a particular church. Due to a church's resident anointing, visiting ministers may find themselves flowing in an area—whether prophetic, healing, miracles, salvation, or preaching—at a level they do not normally flow in.

Resistant. Describes an attitude, a climate, an organization, a person, or anything else that is not receptive and is against something. If you are resistant, you are not easily moved, not easily influenced.

Responsibility. Being "response-able." Whatever you have the ability to respond to, you are responsible for. It is taking of ownership. Responsibility is completely different from blame.

Rest. A position of freedom from conflict and anxiety. To be free from labor and laborious religious things. The Sabbath is referred to as the day of rest because Christ has become our Sabbath. If anyone has entered into Christ, he or she has ceased from labor. The Bible says, "Let us who labor enter that rest." When you are in Christ, you should be at rest. You should not be working, trying to be saved, and trying to be religious. Being at rest means that you are at peace with your environment. You are not in conflict with people. This rest doesn't mean lack of activity, but it means that you are not struggling and laboring to inherit favor with God.

Restoration. To restore is to put something or someone back into a previous place of ownership or authority. Restoration implies that something was lost or damaged and then regained. The book of Galatians says, "If a brother be overtaken in a fault, you who are spiritual restore." In that context, the word restore carries with it the connotation of resetting a broken bone. If a bone is broken, that bone has to be reset. That is a restoring process. It can involve time, pain, and the loss of certain mobility and freedom until it is fully functioning again. This has a spiritual implication. Restoring people spiritually may be painful for them, and you may have to restrict their movement in some way. They may have a loss of freedom for a time until whatever has been spiritually or psychologically broken gets strong and heals. This loss of freedom is like a cast on a broken bone. It limits their movement. When a bone heals, it is actually stronger in the mended place, and if it breaks again, it probably won't break in the same place. You should seek to restore people spiritually so that they will be stronger than they were before. Those who are spiritual should seek to restore; it is not done for pain or for hurt but to make them whole.

Resurrection. A person's coming back to life after being dead.

Revelation. Something that one knows by virtue of spiritual insight. (See Gifts of the Spirit.)

Revelation of the house. The prevailing, understood will of God and its application, purpose, and direction for a particular church. Different pastors may all have similar beliefs, but things that one may do may be the revelation of his particular house because his house functions according to his revealed will and knowledge. This does not necessarily mean that these things are opposed to the will and knowledge of another pastor. It means that one pastor does things one way, and another pastor does things another way.

Reverend. A title conferred upon people by the state when they become licensed as ministers. Reverend is also a title given to members of the clergy to distinguish them.

Revival. A resurgence of spiritual and religious happenings that bring fresh life to believers and that attract unbelievers.

Reward. Although many may have the idea that a reward is payment for services rendered, a reward is not necessarily commensurate with the act. A reward is beyond the *quid pro quo* of an action. (*Quid pro quo* is a Latin term meaning an even exchange.) Reward does imply that something must be done to obtain it, but the reward is larger than what the payment for the services rendered would normally be. When David fought Goliath, Saul said that whoever killed the giant would be rewarded with his daughter. This implies something larger than simply being paid a fee to kill the giant. A reward is also a gift. God told Abraham, "I am your exceedingly great reward." The Bible says, "Without faith it is impossible to please God." Those who come to God must believe that He is a rewarder of those who diligently seek him.

Rhema. Another word for *word*. A *rhema* word is the concept that scriptures may come into the *now* and be immediately relevant for a given person at a particular time. All of a sudden something may jump off the page and just explode on the inside of you, and it is no longer just words on a page. A hundred other people might be reading that same verse around the city, but it became a *rhema* word to you. It is alive. It was breathed out of the mouth of God and exploded on the inside of you. It is God's word to you at that moment in that situation.

Rhythm of life. Rhythm of life is the concept that most of the things God made function according to a rhythm. Your heart beats according to a rhythm. Tides move according to a rhythm. We breathe according to a rhythm. Understanding this concept brings us into harmony with our environment and makes us content in the state we are in because we know our pendulum swings. Things are subject to change. Learning the rhythm of life means learning to be in coordination with times and seasons.

Righteousness. Right standing with God.

Rock. A rock is something that is sure, solid, and immovable. It is used as a descriptive term of the strength, immutability, and foundational qualities of God and His Word.

Rod. A rod in the natural sense is a length of wood that can be held in the hand, but a rod is also symbolic of authority. Moses had a rod that he carried with him when he spoke to Pharaoh and when he divided the Red Sea. The staff of the shepherd brought the sheep close, and the rod was used to beat the wolves away. Rods speak of authority. (See Staff, shepherd's.)

Sabbath. Sabbath means rest and comes from the seventh day, when God ceased from His labors and rested. It speaks of the time of rest. It also speaks of the position that Christians walk in: When we come into Christ, we enter a Sabbath rest. That means that we cease from our laboring to please God in our own efforts, and we enter into the rest of His labor.

Sacrifice. Forfeiting something to obtain a greater gain.

Saints. A biblical definition is the saints of old who died in faith. We sometimes refer to believers in the church as the saints of God. People sometimes refer to each other as saints. It is a term of endearment for the people of God.

Salt. Salt is the concept that Christians are preservatives; we preserve the earth. Also, salt makes you thirsty for something else; it makes you thirsty for water. Being around Christians should make people thirsty for the Living Water.

Salvation. Salvation has past, present, and future tense. For example, I have been saved from the penalty of sin, I am being saved from the power of sin, and I will be saved from the presence of sin. Salvation implies deliverance. It implies a process, but it is also complete. My spirit has been saved. My soul is in the process of being saved, and one day my body will be saved or delivered from the presence of evil. Salvation begins at the born-

141

S

again experience, and it is ongoing, increasing, and progressive.

Sanctification. To sanctify something is to set it apart for God's use and purposes. Sanctification in and of itself will not make you clean. You can't be sanctified unless you are clean. To sanctify is to set apart or to consecrate. Sanctify also means to purify or to clean from sin. To be sanctified, you must be willing to remove anything internally or externally that could hinder you; you must realize that you're not in a right place with God and need to take care of that.

Sanctuary. Used to describe the gathering place of a church, where the main services are conducted. This is different from a children's wing or a gymnasium. In the broader sense, a sanctuary is a place of safety and of preservation from enemies. In a legal sense, ages ago there was the idea of seeking sanctuary. The concept itself means to be preserved and to be set apart.

Saved. (See Salvation and Born again.)

Savior. One of the names or titles given to Jesus Christ.

Second Coming. One of the doctrines of the New Testament, which says that Christ, who left the earth physically and visibly, will return in like manner. The end of this age and the opening of the next age will be signified by the Second Coming of Christ. The Second Coming of Christ will bring us into what is referred to as the Millennial Age, when Christ will rule and reign on the earth for one thousand years.

S

Seducing spirits. A group of spirits who are not overt, but covert, and they seduce people and slowly take them away from the faith, the truth, and the positive in life. People can be seduced when something appears to offer them what they think they want. It is not necessarily a person doing the seducing a lot of times; it can be a spirit. The end effect is that a person begins to lose focus and positive direction. A seducing spirit provides another focus.

See. To perceive. To understand.

Seed. Has several meanings. It involves offspring, which are referred to as your seed. It biologically involves a man's sperm; he sows his seed into a woman. It also involves money, which is sometimes referred to as seed. Ultimately, the concept of seed throughout the Bible involves anything that you release or sow that will produce something after its own kind. You have within you the seed you need to get everything you want. You can set into motion whatever you want by virtue of the seed that you now possess.

Seed faith. A term used in conjunction with prosperity, sowing, and reaping. You do not need to have the faith for your entire harvest if you just have enough faith to sow the seed that will produce that harvest.

Seer. An Old Testament word for prophet. A seer is a visionary. A vision is not necessarily an out-of-body experience. A seer is one who sees things clearly and sees their meanings. For example, when people have discernment or prophetic insight, they do not necessarily see something other than what everyone else sees. A lot of times they see the same thing but in a different way. They see things, their relevance, and their importance, rather than just seeing them in the natural.

Self-control. Self-control is self-government. It is the ability to govern one's self and particularly to have control over the physical and soul areas.

Self-righteous. Describes people who feel they are righteous based on their own merits and works, as opposed to relying upon grace and the work of Christ.

Seminar. A teaching format that is usually organized and very topical. It generally includes handouts, lectures, the use of overhead projectors, and things of that nature.

Send. People are sent when they go somewhere with the authority of another person. For example, some people *go* on mission trips, and some people are *sent* on mission trips. If they are sent, then they go with a blessing, they go with authority, they go with prayer cover, and they go by the bidding of another. The word *apostle* actually comes from the word *sent*. Apostles are the sent ones.

Serpent. With a capital "S," it is a name given to describe the Devil, a demonic power, or unclean spirits.

Servant. A person who does the bidding of another. It may involve a hired position. It has both a positive and a negative implication. The positive implication refers to people who serve the ideas and thoughts of another person because they have a task that they can perform. The negative context refers to someone who is doing something merely for remuneration. This person's heart may not be in it. (See Sons and daughters of God.)

Serve. To do something that will ultimately benefit someone else, especially if done with altruistic motivation. A person who is serving is not looking to be remunerated. To serve is also to execute or to carryout a purpose; an example is "to serve God."

Set times. The word *set* means permanent, fixed, immovable. Genesis talks about how God set the stars into place, and they are fixed in their courses. Set also relates to the effect of concrete; concrete sets and becomes permanent. There are set times, which God knows from beginning to end, for His words to come to pass and for some events to happen. There are set, fixed times for things.

Shadow. One of the ways the Bible is interpreted. Shadow refers to something in the Old Testament that is not necessarily the substance of a thing but is actually the form of something else that occurs later in the New Testament. It is metaphoric. Shadow is picturesque and analogous to something that will be revealed in the New Covenant. It is a precursor, something that comes before. The terms type and shadow work together. For example, David is a type of Christ. The ark can be a type of salvation, and certain things in the Old Testament are a shadow of something in the New Testament. An example is the protection of the blood of the lamb at Passover; it is a shadow of the protection of the blood of Jesus later. Certain things in the Old Covenant are only understood as you see them in that light. Things in the Old

S

Testament shadow or foreshadow certain things in the New Testament. (See Type.)

Sheep. A word used for gatherings of Christians, and Christians in general. Sheep are shepherded and protected against certain predators.

Shepherd. A shepherd is a delineation of leadership. It is a reference to those who oversee the flock (meaning Christians), lead it, guide it, feed it, and protect it. Christ is the Chief Shepherd, and pastors under Him are referred to as undershepherds.

Shouting. Shouting is a form of praise and a response signifying victory.

Sign. A natural, visible occurrence that points to something else and that generally indicates a spiritual event or truth.

Signify. A sign indicates (or signifies) a spiritual event or truth.

Signs and wonders. Signs and wonders are supernatural occurrences that follow the lives of believers and those who walk by faith. A sign points to something greater than itself, and a wonder causes people to ponder. Signs and wonders are unusual occurrences that cause people to look to the source of those events.

Sin. There is the nature of sin, the state of sin, and the act of sin. People are born into a sin nature, which means that by their nature people will gravitate toward wrong. The act of sin is transgressing God's law. The state of sin is what people live in if they sin habitually. Adam opened the world to the sin nature, and Adam reproduced after his own kind; therefore, since the fall of Adam, people by their nature have been evil. What changes that nature is being born again.

Sinai. The mountain from which the law came. It is tied with law and legalism. The move from Sinai to Zion is a type and shadow. The church moved from the legalism of Sinai to Zion, the place of God's dwelling, peace, and blessing—the place of spiritual things.

Singing. Vocalizing words set to music and melody. It is one of the distinctions of praise and worship.

Sinner. A person who lives with a sin nature. A person who is still bound by the sin nature. A person who has been saved is not still a sinner. You are not a sinner saved by grace; you *used to be* a sinner, and you were saved by grace. Once you are saved, you are no longer a sinner. As the Bible says, you are a new creature in Christ Jesus. God makes you into a new creature, a new being. Sinners repent for who they are. Christians repent for what they do. A sinner is still bound by the fallen nature, unregenerate, and not born again. Christians do not live in the nature of sin, nor should they live in the state of sin; however, Christians can commit the act of sin.

Among the acts of sin, there are sins of omission, sins of commission, and sins of degree. There are some things that you should do that you don't do. There are some things that you shouldn't do but you do anyway. And there are other things that in and of themselves are not

S

sin, but taken to excess they are sin. It is not a sin to eat, but it is a sin to be a glutton. The Bible teaches that people are not sinners because they sin. They sin because they *are* sinners. Because that is their nature, that is their fruit. People do not become righteous by doing right things, but rather they become righteous and then do right. It is a difference of nature. The difference between religiosity's dead works and being born again is a changed nature. That's why we use the term born again; it is to be born from above. It is not working your way into a position at which your debits and credits equal out or at which your good works outweigh your bad works. This position describes a person who still has a fallen nature but tries to do enough right things to not seem like a sinner. But when people become born again, their nature changes; then that which comes out of them will automatically change. They will want to do the right things and will begin to live out the right things because their nature has changed.

Sister. A term of endearment given to female members of the church body.

Skill. The ability to do something well. People's level of skill determines their ability to do something.

Song. Words and melodies set to music. Singing and songs are used in praise and worship.

Song of the Lord. Prophetic and spontaneous in nature. It is singing to a congregation or over people what you hear from God in your heart and spirit. It is not sung *to* God. It is sung *from* God. It is the song of the Lord; it belongs to Him. The Bible says that the Lord your God rejoices over you with singing. So the song of the Lord is His singing back to people. The song of the Lord conveys to people in music and song the interpretation of what someone has heard in the Spirit.

Sons and daughters of God. The position into which people who believe in Christ are brought. It distinguishes people with a servant mentality from people coming into maturity as sons and daughters. Sons and daughters do not function based on fear of God in the negative sense and are not just functioning on principles and laws of the kingdom. They have received the inheritance of the kingdom and by their nature obey the laws because they are part of the family. The term *servant* here is likened to religiosity, and the term sons and daughters is associated with spiritual things.

Soul. The seat of the personality. It contains the emotions, mind, will, intellect, and memories.

Soul tie. Refers to your emotions, mind, will, intellect, memories, and personality being entangled with or adversely influenced by someone else. This tie occurs when the soul is improperly influenced, misdirected, and altered by a relationship with someone. A soul tie is undue influence. (See Ahab spirit.)

Soulical. Those things that belong to the realm of the soul.

Sovereign. Having supreme rank and power. Sovereign speaks of God's position in the universe. He is unmatched. He is able to do what He wants, when He wants, how He wants, and with whom He wants. He needs no advice, counsel, permission, or forewarning.

Speak into one's life. This concept involves both the giving and the accepting of counsel. Speaking into the life of someone means that you are giving advice or wisdom. Allowing someone to speak into your life means that you are willing to accept or to consider that person's counsel and advice. You should be very careful to accurately assess the understanding, motivations, awareness, and gifts of those you allow to speak into your life.

Spirit. Your spirit is the real you, the eternal you, the highest order of who people are. It is the part of you created in the image of God. It is one of the three parts of man. (See Three parts of man.)

Spirit-filled. Used colloquially to refer to the baptism of the Holy Spirit and to the infilling of the Holy Spirit. It generally means a person has received a second definite work of grace. Its evidence is speaking in tongues. A Spirit-filled person is open to the gifts of the Spirit and to the miraculous. (See Baptism of the Holy Spirit and Gifts of the Spirit.)

Spirit-led. To know something and have internal witness on something due to the internal working of the Holy Spirit within you. When you are Spirit-led, you do not require a lot of natural confirmation.

Spirit of. When people have the spirit of something, they exhibit the state, nature, or qualities of that spirit. A spirit is transferable and discernible. This can be positive or negative. It is positive when we say that someone

S

has the spirit of Elijah, and we mean that the person is bold, confrontational, or prophetic. It is negative when we say that someone has the spirit of Ahab, and we mean that the person is weak, wicked, or abducting. It could also be said that the spirit of destruction or gossip or perversion is on people, meaning they carry these qualities and can transfer them to other people. A person could also have the spirit of revival, restoration, or revelation.

Spirit of alarm. A spirit that a person carries that causes his or her communication to produce a response of panic, terror, or trauma in the listener. This spirit can arouse a person to undue alarm or fear.

Spirit of antichrist. A spirit that is against anything of God, against anything positive, and against anything attached to God, Christ, or the anointing. Even some religious spirits are antichrist. They are against the truth, the true relationship with God, and true anointing. The spirit of antichrist is not like the spirit of the age, which can be very covert and subtle. Usually the antichrist spirit is overt. Like any spirit, the spirit of antichrist has to find physical bodies to carry out its desired effect on earth. The effect of an antichrist spirit depends upon who gets it and who has it. If an antichrist spirit gets on a charismatic leader, through the law of association and transference of spirits, the spirit will be able to push certain philosophies and mindsets to other people. Eventually the leader of a nation could be engulfed in the spirit of antichrist. The spirit of antichrist began with some other spiritual being and now continues to be transferred, much like a virus. This spirit is ultimately upheld by real entities. Certain political ideologies work better than others do with the spirit of antichrist.

Spirit of bondage. Something that people do not want to be constrained by, yet they are unable, or at least feel themselves unable, to be free from it. Bondage is anything that you no longer feel in control of; it holds you in a particular spot in your life and limits your freedom. The spirit of bondage keeps this condition working in your life.

Spirit of death. Desires to bring about death and destruction. Sometimes when you go to a hospital room, you may notice a spirit of death there. The person is perhaps not really supposed to die, but he or she has entertained or received the spirit of death. If you enter that hospital room with greater authority, you can bind the spirit of death and cast it out. The spirit of death is working in school shootings. This spirit can get into people's minds. It tries to get someone to facilitate an atmosphere in which it can work its cause, which is ultimately death and destruction. The father behind this is Lucifer.

Spirit of divination. Divination is using a method to try to foretell the will of God; it is fortune telling, and a spirit can carry it. In fortune telling, by the way, somebody is making a fortune by telling you something; for example, they make four dollars per minute on a 900 number.

Spirit of error. If a person has a spirit of error, even if you speak truth to them, by the time they get done processing it, it comes out erroneous. Not everyone that makes a mistake, though, has a spirit of error. Some people are just dense. But a spirit of error will take truth and miss the mark with it. It is a spirit that causes a person not to be able to properly comprehend and/or apply truth.

Spirit of fear. Causes people to be paralyzed emotionally, to be overactive physically or emotionally, and to make decisions and movements based upon an exaggerated or false perception of reality.

Spirit of haughtiness. It is like pride, but it is not just pride. It is a mixture of pride and arrogance. Haughtiness is the spirit that causes people to appear and feel superior while also being aloof and condescending to others. Pride and haughtiness are self-focused. Pride says, "I am big," but haughtiness says, "I am big, and you are little."

Spirit of heaviness. Includes depression and other things that hold a person down or under.

Spirit of infirmity. An evil spirit that desires to bring the manifestation of sickness and disease.

Spirit of jealousy. An evil spirit that causes a person to feel unduly and disproportionately threatened by someone else receiving attention, position, or recognition. The spirit makes people feel as if they are being replaced. This spirit can also make people feel threatened by circumstances. (See Envy.)

Spirit of offense. There are people who always seem to be offended. When people are always offended, it is easy for the Devil to lay a trap for them because they are always going to take the bait. When they do take the bait, they become ensnared by it. The offense that people feel is not the trap; the perception of offense is the bait. The word *offense* comes from a word that describes the part of a trap that holds the bait. The concept here is that when people become offended, they have put their hand on the bait in the trap, and they are about to be ensnared because they fell for it. They let themselves be offended.

Look how this functions in people's lives. They are getting ready for a promotion, or they go to a new job. During the first day, something happens because that's what they set themselves up for. They won't be able to succeed in that job because they have become offended. Psalm 116 says, "Great peace have they that love Thy law. Nothing shall offend them." If you understand the principles and plans of God and love the way God's plan and kingdom work, you can't be offended because you will not allow anyone to offend you. You won't take the bait. (See also Assigned spirits and spiritual assassins.)

Spirit of poverty. Poverty is a spirit that causes people's resources to be devoured. This spirit holds people under, produces victimized mentality, and keeps people in continual lack. Being broke, on the other hand, is a temporary economic condition. The spirit of poverty is continual.

Spirit of the age. A prevailing mindset that functions as a collective consciousness of certain groups of people that are living at a particular time. However, not everyone alive at a given time necessarily adopts or operates from that mindset.

Spirit of the Lord. Another term used to refer to the Holy Spirit or to the essence of who God is.

Spirit of the wolf. Used to describe people who attempt to separate some people from others, especially from headship ministry and from those in authority. When people are away from protective authority figures, proper relationships, and proper cover, these spirits can harm them and ultimately devour them.

Spiritual. In its generic form, it means being aware of things that are of the Spirit. Spiritual people are mature and have an understanding of certain spiritual principles. They are not novices but are versed and grown and stable in spiritual matters. The Bible says that those of you who are spiritual seek to restore people. If you understand what is beyond the natural and if you have certain principles in place, you do the right things. Spiritual involves things beyond the soul and physical realms.

Spiritual climates. Involve the discernible atmosphere relating to the receptivity to the Gospel in general and related truths specifically. An atmosphere is the unseen yet discernible presence of the dominant spirit in a region, church, or city. Atmospheres that are sustained create climates. Governing churches are in part called to be the stewards of climates by creating and sustaining an atmosphere conducive for the Holy Spirit's work.

Spiritual prostitution. Prostitution means that a person will lay with whoever will pay. Spiritual prostitution is the concept that people will use their gifts and abilities, get under someone, or be under someone's authority or headship only for monetary things or for what can be gotten. In such cases, there is no true covenant. For example, someone who is talented to lead music at a church may not care whose church it is or what the pastor preaches; this person would have no real relationship with the pastor. This musician may stay three weeks or three months, but when somebody else offers twice the salary, the musician will go there. A person with this spirit doesn't care whom they get under or whom they are having intercourse with as long as the money is right. It is prostituting gifts and abilities without relationship or covenant, and there is a lack of headship and authority.

Spiritual song. A spontaneous, original song that springs from an internal origin. A spiritual song is something you sing to God.

Spiritual warfare. Engaging evil spiritual forces in combat. In the spiritual world, there are spirits, demons, and spiritual forces working against our progress, our goals, and humanity. Spiritual warfare involves the things that pertain to engaging those spirits in conflict and battle.

Staff, ministry. All people who serve under the governmental head of a ministry to fulfill the ministry purposes.

Staff, shepherd's. Used by the shepherd to pull a sheep close and away from harm. The shepherd's rod was used to beat the wolves away. A staff in the figurative sense brings people close. It is comforting.

Steadfast. To be consistent, unwavering, and continually moving forward in your convictions and beliefs.

Step of faith. The concept that faith demands a corresponding action. In the New Testament, James said, "Faith without works is dead." Every belief demands a corresponding action. A step of faith is an action you take due to your deep convictions and internal beliefs, and this action may not be explainable otherwise. This step is a physical action based on faith that you are going in the right direction and walking in the light of God.

Stewards. Because God is the ultimate owner of all things, He has not placed people in a position of ownership but in a position of stewardship. Stewards operate under authority and ultimately have to give an account for what they did with what they had.

Stewardship. The position of life wherein one understands that they are to give an account to someone of greater authority for their actions or their possession of something. Man gives an account to God for his stewardship of the earth. Stewardship is also a generic term that is sometimes used when one talks about church finances.

Storm. A position in life at which things around you are uncomfortable and become contrary to your destination and your faith.

Strength. The measure of your energy, endurance, and fortitude. The Bible says that if your faith faints in the day of adversity, then your strength is small. For

S

strength to be genuinely strong, it has to start strong and endure over time.

Strife. The spirit at work where there are contentions and warring opinions. It can be an atmosphere or an attitude. Strife does not necessarily have to have a topic. If a person wants to be in strife with you or to create strife with you, the strife can tear the relationship. Once strife is there, it may invade other issues.

Strongholds. Attitudes and ways of thinking that have been accepted and operated under for years. Strongholds are based upon demonic forces, faulty understanding, or ignorance. They are actually thought processes that make people feel that this is the way things will always be. These influences become strong over a period of time, hence the term *stronghold*. Strongholds can operate in individuals and cover peoples, groups, or cities that have a common collective consciousness on a particular matter. A spirit of poverty in an area, for example, frequently stays in that area. Government programs don't change it. People being delivered from poverty have certain strongholds in their mind, such as the victim mentality that says, "Somebody owes me something. I would be this, but I am stuck being that." There is a certain process that causes them to believe that. The person held in that mentality or behind that wall is in a stronghold. The stronghold holds the person. Strongholds are referred to as such because they are not the easiest things to break. Breaking them takes some disassembling and some attacking. Stronghold is part of warfare terminology.

158

Strongman. Used to describe the devil, the ruling spirit, or the prevalent mentality that keeps people in bondage.

Stupid. Ignorance is not knowing something. Stupidity is knowing something and choosing to overlook it. Stupid people act in a state of ignorance by going forward without acknowledging that they are *in* a state of ignorance. They go forward blindly. Stupidity is an unwillingness or inability to actually look at something; it is misjudging things. People who are stupid don't bother to correctly inform themselves. Stupidity is the bane of civilization and spiritual enlightenment.

Submission. Willfully giving yourself to those of greater authority. It involves both application and attitude. A submissive attitude does not resist or rebel against those in the place of headship and government in the body or in the family. Submission in action is living out of the authority of others. Submission is not weakness. In the true definition, submission is not forced. There is a difference between submission and compliance. The difference is attitude.

Supernatural. Describes spiritual happenings that are above the natural, material world. The supernatural can be positive or negative. Supernatural happenings belong to the spirit world rather than to the natural world.

Supernatural ministry. The part of the ministry that belongs to the realm of the spirit. It is the part that is not definable by natural terms. There are certain things that just happen because they are in the supernatural aspect of the ministry. There are certain things that happen in services that people may not even be aware of, things that nobody orchestrated or planned. These supernatural happenings are not really products of the singing, the preaching, the carpet, or the ushers. They are spiritual. Supernatural ministry could also be used to define the ministry of people who operate in that zone regularly.

Sword of the Spirit. A term given to define the Bible, the Word of God.

Tabernacle. Moveable and impermanent, a tent. Several tabernacles are mentioned in the Bible, and they were all mobile. They were mobile tents in which worship was performed and in which the Spirit of God dwelt. Figuratively speaking, Christians are tabernacles of the Holy Spirit. I John says, "The Word became flesh and dwelt among us." The word *dwelt* there is the same word for *tabernacle.* Another translation could say that "the Word *tabernacled* among us." The children of Israel had a feast of tabernacles, at which they stayed in tents for a certain number of days to remind themselves of how they came out of the wilderness.

Tail. The tail of something is not self-directed. The tail is the opposite of the head. The head speaks of government, authority, and decision-making. Being the tail means being dragged around. It means being the last. God's promise is that you will be the head and not the tail. The Word says that you will be above only and not beneath.

Talents. The natural manifestation of the gifts that God gives us. A talent is the ability to do a certain thing. A talent was also a measure of money in biblical times.

Tares. Comes from the parable of the wheat and tares. Tares look like wheat. They grow together with wheat, but they are discarded on the threshing room floor after the harvest. Metaphorically, tares mean imitation Christians—imitation righteous people. These people

T

stand alongside and mirror the actions or words of righteous Christians but are not true in their heart. (See Threshing floor.)

Teachable. Understanding that there is yet more you can know. The desire and willingness to receive instruction.

Teacher. Someone who has expertise concerning certain information and who is capable and willing to instruct others.

Teaching. (See Train and Instruction.)

Temperance. Self-control. The ability to be moderate and to not be ruled by your emotions. (See Fruit of the Spirit.)

Temptation. Something that appears gratifying and pulls you away from a predetermined, good plan. It replaces something good with something that is of a lower nature, drawing your attention away from your focus. It is also the process by which you move through those enticing circumstances. Temptation plagues the body and the soul.

Territorial spirits. Spirits assigned to particular geographical regions; they produce a climate that tolerates and accepts their influence. For example, you may find that some poor people move more often than other people do, but they never go very far. They may move again and again but stay in the same small area. Some poverty-bound people get checks from the government that are good for any neighborhood in town. The government pays for rent anywhere, yet some people stay in the same neighborhood because a spirit holds them there—a territorial spirit. The Bible says that the oppression of the poor man is his poverty, which means that some poor people are oppressed because they don't strive to get out of their downward cycle of poverty. For example, there might be a little corner store down the street from them. That little corner store charges them ten times more than another store, but they will not go anywhere else because a territorial spirit tells them, "This is your neighborhood. This is where you should shop. This is where you should do all your business." There are areas in every town where the police know the drug buys happen. The prostitutes frequent these areas. If the police know that this is where the majority of crimes take place, you may wonder why these things still happen there. The reason is that territorial spirits hold those areas.

Test. A situation in life when people who have been taught are called on to show what they have learned. Some people think that tests occur to teach something. People are not tested until they have been taught. A test is *not* to teach you something. The test indicates that you have *already* been taught something. You don't get a test on the first day of school. You first get the material, and *then* you get the test. Life is also that way. When you enter a test, you have already been taught whatever you need to know to succeed. The test evaluates your faith to see if you know how to apply what you have learned. You should know what to do. Take drug addicts, for example. Their continued drug use is not a test. However, if they change their point of view, stop abusing drugs, and then are presented with a chance to do drugs again, that opportunity becomes a test. They know what they should

T

do. The drugs are the temptation, and the situation with their old friends is the test.

Testimony. Your story. The word *testimony* comes from *test*. It means that you had a positive outcome, and now you want to share how you were victorious in your test. The purpose of a testimony is to encourage and to strengthen someone else. It is a personalized version of how the Word of God has been applied in your life. Every person's testimony is in many ways unique. A testimony is sharing God's triumph in your particular circumstances.

Testing. The circumstances by which learning is tested. When information has been given to you, it must be tested or proved. Testing proves information as fire refines gold. It removes impurities from your belief systems so that what remains after the test is more pure. For your belief systems and principles to be fully comprehended and trusted, they have to be tested. (See Trial and Test.)

The Adversary. The Devil.

Theocracy. A method of governing by which God rules in earthly government. The children of Israel, for example, were under a theocracy. The church is a kingdom, and God is the king. The church is ultimately a theocracy.

Thirst. An intense desire for something.

Three parts of man. The spiritual, which is a person's highest state; the soul, which embodies the emotions,

T

thoughts, and feelings; and the body, which is the flesh vehicle of humanity on earth.

Threshing floor. The place where bundles of wheat were taken after they were harvested. The threshing floor was a flat, circular surface with a net under it. The bundles were thrown up in the air when the wind came. The tares would blow away, and the wheat would fall back to the net. In the Bible, events happened on certain threshing floors, and they were times of separation. A threshing floor is a place of sifting. Metaphorically, it is a place where those things that are not profitable to your life are blown away. This is not always a pleasant process because there may be beating, trampling, and winds involved. Jesus made the famous statement to Peter: "I pray for you that your faith will not fail because Satan has desired to sift you as wheat." He never said that He was going to stop the process. He said, "I pray for you that your faith will not fail." In other words, your adversary has come, and he desires to sift you; however, if you go through this process, the only thing that he can take from you is that which you do not need anyway. You will be purified afterward. (See Tares.)

Tithe. The word *tithe* means tenth. It is the first ten percent of any monetary increase that a person receives.

Tithing. Tithing is the act of returning ten percent to God through the agency of the church. Returning through the church is an integral part of the process.

Titles/Title of. The importance of titles is that they distinguish and identify the position and function of someone in the body, as well as that person's relationship to

you. A ministry gift can be more effective when it is identified and recognized. You should not confer a title upon
yourself. Rather, those of authority confirm a function,
publicly recognize the function, and then refer to the person in that function by a title.

Token. A small, insignificant representation of what
should be.

Tongues. (See Gifts of the Spirit.)

Touch. Not physical touch. The concept of touch
referred to here is reaching someone and making contact. You can touch someone with a song. You can touch
someone with your words. Touch speaks of something
making a connection. We refer to touching someone,
touching a city, and touching the world. Touching is
making an effect by reaching and making a connection.

Touch and agree. A concept of prayer. Jesus said, "If
any two of you on earth shall touch and agree it shall be
done." The touching in this instance is the physical
aspect of what you do; the agreeing is the conceptual or
spiritual aspect. Your agreement is conceptual, theological, and spiritual. The touching is the practical aspect of
how you do it. If two people are going to touch and agree
that something should be done, then they come into an
agreement, a oneness of mind, that this is what should
be done. But they could still lose their agreement and
the effectiveness of their prayers if they don't agree on
the touching part of it, which is *how* it should be done.
If you can agree conceptually and spiritually and if you
can agree on the touching—how it should be done—then
whatever you ask God shall be done on earth. The agree-

ing is the coming together spiritually; the touching is the execution.

Train. Training is different from teaching because teaching is informational only. Training involves having the students do again and again what they have been taught. First, the information is demonstrated to the student, and then the student executes the action under oversight. You can't be trained to bowl by having someone bowl in front of you all the time. At some point, *you* have to bowl. But your bowling is with the teacher watching. Training involves students' executing something while under authority so that they can learn how it should be done. This involves instruction and teaching, but training is primarily the hands-on part. (See Teaching and Instruction.)

Transference of spirits. Can be positive or negative. Through communication, fellowship, and relationship, the weaker will receive from the stronger, and what one person carries in the way of spirit and attitude can be conveyed and transferred into the life of another. With this point in mind, you need to be careful with whom you associate because this transference can happen with or without your agreement. (See Spirit of.)

Transgression. To transgress is to step off the path of good and to work against the law of God. It is purposely stepping against the law of God or stepping off the path of right and stepping in another direction.

Travail. Travail is usually associated with childbirth, but metaphorically it is a word that is especially used in regard to prayer or to anything to which you conceptually give birth. It refers to the rigors of childbirth and the pain that is endured for the joy that will come. The moments of pressing when everything becomes uncomfortable are usually greatest before the birth or the arrival of the vision, dream, or goal. Travail is not part of testing.

Trees. There is the natural definition, but trees are symbolic in the Bible and stand for different things. Sometimes Christians are referred to as trees of righteousness.

Trespass. An offense.

Trial. A test or storm. A test is frequently a more immediate sort of thing (testing the waters). A trial is something that needs greater endurance and greater perseverance to overcome. It generally has a longer duration than a test. A trial also has opposition in it. A test can be very subjective. An event can be a test for one person but not necessarily for another person. In a trial, a person's subjective feelings are not the only thing involved; there are other people and things in opposition, such as there would be in a court trial.

Trinity. The Trinity refers to the Father, the Son, and the Holy Spirit. (See Tripartite.)

Tripartite. Conveys the same concept as Trinity. Some people refer to it as the Holy Trinity, the Tripartite God, the Triune, or the Godhead. Those are all words used to define the Father, the Son, and the Holy Spirit and their relation, unity, and function with each other.

Triune. See Tripartite.

Truth. The ultimate reality. Truth is what actually *is*.

Type. Something that represents another thing (type and shadow). Certain things in the Old Testament are considered types of things in the New Testament. (See Shadow.)

Unbelief. Unbelief is cynicism about God. It is not the lack of faith. It is a decided position that is hostile toward God; it is a determination to be cynical and critical. Unbelief is a decision not to believe. Doubt is being unsure. Unbelief is a position.

Unchurched. Describes people who have not received the Word of God in their heart and formed a committed relationship with Him.

Universal church. A term used to describe as a whole all people who belong to Christ, all people who are saved.

Unruly. People who buck the system are unruly. They get off the beaten path and live their life in a way other than what they have been taught.

Unteachable. The disposition of being unreceptive to instruction, counsel, or authority.

Upper Room. The Upper Room is the place in Acts 2 where the Holy Spirit was poured out upon the apostles and others on the Day of Pentecost. It is an actual, physical place in a building in Israel. It connotes the highest level of life also. It can speak of the highest person that you are. God does not deal with you in your lowest nature, in your basement; He deals with you in your upper room, in your spirit man.

U

Usher. A person who serves in the church in a variety of areas: helping people find seats, maintaining the order of church services, helping catch those who fall while they are being prayed for, and collecting offerings. In general, ushers are of aid to the people who come to a church service, and ushers assist in any way they can those who are gathered. In some churches, ushers are called porters. (See Ministry of helps.)

Vain imaginations. Thoughts and precepts in the mind that are outside the scope of truth; they ultimately place people at odds with Scripture.

Valley. A low place of life. A time when people do not feel as if they are on top of things.

Variance. Altering instruction. Varying from what you have been told to do. Variance is like a spirit or an attitude that people carry. When they are given something to do, they always have to alter it. They change it and introduce some characteristic of their own to pervert it or to flavor it in some way. This is an absolutely negative thing. You may ask somebody to do something as part of a bigger program, but this person won't see the big program. People with variance see things as being *their* program and go about changing instructions as they see fit. This tends to keep the big program from coming to fruition. If people are really on board in an organization, they will do their best to execute their orders exactly as they have been instructed.

Veil. The concept that some things are hidden from casual observance. Something that is veiled takes further investigation. There is something great behind the veil if you will do what is necessary to get behind it. The Holy of Holies was behind a veil. The Bible says that the veil that hid the Holy of Holies was physically torn from top to bottom the moment Christ died. That veil's being

V

torn was symbolic of Christ's removing the veil that separated people from the Holy of Holies, meaning God.

Vessel. In the natural, a container that something is put into. Also, we are referred to as earthen vessels. There are vessels of gold, silver, clay, and earth. Vessel is a delineation given to people that means they contain something more valuable than themselves.

Victory. The positive outcome of a battle, trial, test, or adversity. Victory also is a state of being in which people confidently maintain assurance that all is well and that all will be well.

Vine. A descriptive term for Christ. He said, "I am the vine; you are the branches." We are the branches, so we get our life and our strength from Him.

Virtue. Used in a couple of different ways in the Bible; there are virtuous women, and we should remain virtuous. A person of virtue is one of propriety, one of good standing, and one of high morals. There is also another concept involving virtue. A woman in the Bible touched the hem of Jesus' garment in order to be healed, and as she did so, He became aware that virtue had left him. Goodness and healing and what she needed left him and entered her. His virtue went into her.

Vision. A goal. Its spiritual implication is being able to see an outcome before it arrives—to see something internally. A vision and a dream are somewhat different; a vision is more active, and a dream comes to you. A dream is something occurring now or something that will occur in the future. A vision, on the other hand, is something that you have to make happen. If you have a vision, you must begin to work toward making it come to fruition.

Visionary. A person who has vision and is able to impart it to others.

Visitation/habitation of God. When someone has a heightened sense that God is working in his or her life, especially for a particular period of time, this working of God could be referred to as a visitation of God. A church could go through five or six weeks of a heightened sense that God is there, and many people are being born again; miracles are happening. This can be referred to as a visitation. The problem with a visitation is that it is just a visit, and it comes to an end. The ultimate desire is for God to move us from visitation to habitation, which means that God does not just visit us at a heightened level for a small period of time. Habitation means that He dwells with us. He makes His abode with us, and He is always with us.

Voice of God. It can be heard in many ways: through singing, through testimony, through preaching, through circumstances, through a child's speaking, through a song on the radio. When you hear the voice of God, you are made to know the mind of God in a clear way. It doesn't always have to be by external circumstances. God also can speak to your heart. All these things are the voice of God. Another definition of the voice of God refers to how God walked in the garden in Adam's day. It wasn't necessarily an outside source. The voice of God is the term used to describe the way we hear God when He speaks to us. This is similar to the Holy Spirit.

V

Vow. To swear or to make an oath. It is a verbal concept, and it has a financial aspect biblically: to vow a vow. Pledge is not really a biblical term. Vow is a biblical term. You vow that you are going to do something.

Walk. A person's walk of life can be described as the path that he or she is on. Your walk is your progression and your manner of life.

Walk of faith. Speaks of the way of faith, the path of faith that people are on, the actions and steps of faith, and all of the things that are implied with that.

Walking in the Spirit. The daily living of your life from the inside out, rather than from the outside in. When you walk in the Spirit, you apply spiritual principles to the material world.

Walls. Mental constructions that hold some things behind and other things outside. Walls, in the negative sense, are ways of thinking and are generally psychological and of the soul. A lot of times walls are things that people have become socialized in. Sometimes walls can come up almost as a knee-jerk reaction to input from others. For example, you could be talking to someone when a wall comes up; it has become a barrier. In a positive sense, walls can also be used for protection and security. The Bible says, "A man that does not rule his own spirit is like a city whose walls are torn down," which means that anything can rush in upon him. In the kingdom of God, your wall is salvation, and your gate is praise. A gate allows you to get safely inside the wall. This is a word picture of entering into the gate of salvation and being surrounded by walls of protection. Walls speak of life in Christ; He is our wall of protection, and

W – Z

His teachings are ways and consistent precepts that guard against our being run over by emotions or circumstances.

Water. A type and a shadow that represent the spirit world because it is not fixed; it is in motion and has a current and a flow. You can reach into it, and your hand will be wet; however, you can't hold it because it has depth and is unsearchable. There is a correlation between how the earth was made and how people were made. The earth is one-third land and two-thirds water, and people also are that way. People were constructed like the earth; we are one-third that which comes from the earth and two-thirds that which cannot be seen—the soul and the spirit. Water is also symbolic of the Word of God in the Bible. We wash ourselves with the water of the Word. This concept gives us the word picture of walking through the world and accumulating dust and dirt. We use water to wash off all that. As we live our lives, we accumulate thoughts, ideas, pressures, and just the general things of this life, but when we hear the Word of God, it washes those things from us.

Waves. In the positive and historical sense, waves can be used to describe moves of God or the tides, ebbs, and flows of the Holy Spirit. In many places in the Bible, the Holy Spirit has a correlation to water and to the sea and rivers because there is a tide, ebb, current, and flow to it. Sometimes the Spirit of God will move in what can be referred to as waves. In the negative sense, waves are used to describe whatever beats against the boat of your faith; during metaphorical storms in your life, the water in your environment is not smooth. Also in the negative sense, waves are aggravation and environments contrary to where you are going.

Wayside. Describes the discarded places of life, the places of rejection, and the places of hardness that make sowing seeds difficult.

Weakness. An area of deficiency.

Weapons. Tools available to people for combating their enemy. The weapons of our warfare are not carnal, but they are mighty through God. Singing is a weapon against your enemies. Prayer can be a weapon. A weapon can be any tool that you use.

Weapons of warfare. Used when engaging evil spirits in battle so that believers are not defenseless. There are things that can be done to cause certain effects. For example, the blood of Jesus is a weapon of our warfare. Praying in the Spirit, confessing, using the Scripture, fasting, and praying are all weapons of warfare. They are things used for effect upon the spirits that we are engaging in battle.

Weary. Weary is not sleepy. It is becoming internally tired and coming to the point of exhaustion where you are ready to give up.

Well. A state of wholeness. The absence of disease. Being well is bigger than having your physical ailments remedied. It is the entire spiritual man's being at peace, being at rest, and being whole.

Wheat. Symbolic of the children of the kingdom.

W – Z

Whole. Not being fragmented. It is being put together properly.

Wicked. Describes people who are perverted and turned toward things of darkness; these people oppose what is right. Wicked can be used to describe people, such as a wicked person, or a group of people, such as the wicked in the earth.

Wife. The counterpart of a husband. A wife is the female part of the marriage union. (See Helpmeet.)

Wilderness or desert. The times or places of life at which things are dry. Things die in the wilderness or desert. Deserts are rough times, lean times, times of testing and trials.

Wind. Comes from the word for breath and for spirit. When the Holy Spirit came, there was the sound of a mighty rushing wind. Wind speaks of the moving of the Spirit, and it can be likened unto the Spirit.

Wine. Used in the Bible as a type of the Holy Spirit. When the believers on the Day of Pentecost received the infilling of the Holy Spirit, the men in the town thought that these believers were drunk with wine. The believers said, "No, this is that which the prophet Joel prophesied about." Jesus talked about new wine in old wineskins. The term is used several ways. One way is medicinally. Alcohol was poured into a wound to disinfect it, so there is a cleansing element to this term. No matter what the wound or hurt is, the application of the wine, or the Holy Spirit, cleanses it. Wine also has the ability to alter your personality. Metaphorically, this means that people become more joyful, more prone to sing, and more receptive of others when they have received the new wine of the Holy Spirit. The wine used in communion symbolizes the cleansing and the changing power of Christ's blood.

Wineskin. A metaphorical understanding that involves the concepts and administration by which we contain the flow of God in our lives. As old wineskins are brittle and rigid, so many times we become set in our ways or stuck in our thinking. New wine (new flows of the Spirit) demands new wineskins (new ways of thinking and administrating what God is doing). New wineskins are flexible and pliable.

Wisdom. The ability to properly apply knowledge.

Witchcraft. The practice of relating to unclean spirits. An unclean spirit is the same as any other kind of demon. It is a spirit with a perverse ultimate plan. It is against good and distorts truth. The term *unclean spirits* is used because you feel unclean when you get around certain spirits. This is more of a spiritual discerning than it is a natural feeling. You can sense the ugliness of an unclean spirit.

Witness. Someone who has personal knowledge of something and is called upon to give testimony to it. Sometimes someone in church will ask, "Can I get a witness?" This question means that if you know that what is being said is true in your life, then you ought to say so. If you know truth was spoken, you should bear witness to it because the truth is on trial in front of people who don't know the truth. Witness also describes the Holy Spirit's affirmation of something in our spirit.

W – Z

World. Sometimes a distinction is made between the world and the earth, and sometimes these words are used interchangeably. In some contexts, the word *world*, which comes from the word *cosmos*, refers to the system by which people on the earth function. It is the world's system. Jesus said, "He that loves the world knows not the love of the Father. Come out from amongst the world and be ye separate." This obviously does not refer to the earth because the earth is the Lord's. So this speaks of the downward system—not the positive parts—by which the people of the earth function.

Worldly. Carnal. Earthly. Describes a person who carries the qualities of the world, not those of the Spirit.

Worship. Attitudes or actions that ascribe value to who God is.

Wounded spirit. Someone who has been hurt internally and has not gained healing or composure may develop a wounded spirit. This term goes hand in hand with defeated spirit. People who have a wounded spirit may have been violated, disappointed, or so pressed in on that they are hurt and will continue to carry the hurt with them, rendering them somewhat paralyzed in certain areas. (See Defeated spirit and Spirit of offense.)

Wrath. Involves anger. Wrath is anger exhibited, rather than anger internalized. It is anger doing something. To incur someone's wrath is not just to make someone mad. If a person is wrathful, he or she is actually taking action with the anger. Wrath is anger in motion.

Yoke. Joins things together. The concept of a yoke involves animals plowing the field. The yoke went around their necks to harness them together so that they could pull the plow or their load. To be unequally yoked means to go into captivity or covenant with someone who is not going in the same direction, is of a different nature, has different goals and purposes, or is of a different strength level. When the yoke is unequal, one is pulling all the weight, and the other is pulling no weight or is going in another direction. There is an interesting scripture in the Old Testament that says, "You shall not plow your field with an ox and an ass together because it is an unequal yoke." You can't yoke an ox with an ass and expect to get a good result. This interesting scripture involves a type and a shadow. The oxen are servants and are used for sacrifices for worship, and the ass is rebellious and stubborn and self-willed; they cannot be equally yoked. (See Missionary dating.)

Zeal. Akin to the word *fire*. Zeal and fire have their etymology in the same word. To have zeal is to burn with enthusiasm and excitement.

Zion. The place of spiritual dwelling. It is the higher life. It is the Spirit life. It also speaks collectively of the people who live the Spirit life. It is the place from which God rules the earth. In the Old Testament, Zion was a natural geographical location, the place of the king, the habitation of the temple, and the place of rulership and authority. The spiritual meaning is thus transferred to those who have entered the kingdom through spiritual life and are proclaiming God's rulership throughout the earth.